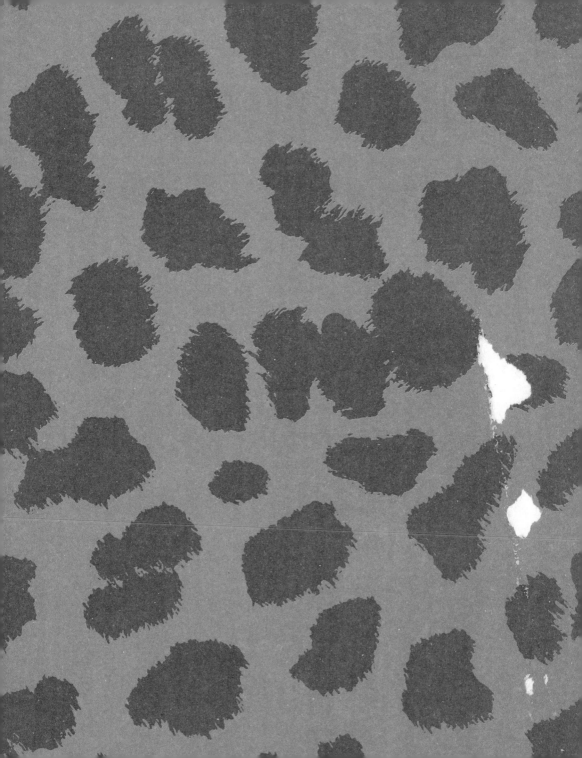

Poodles

AMY FERNANDEZ

Poodles

Project Team
Editor: Stephanie Fornino
Copy Editor: Neal Pronek
Indexer: Lucie Haskins
Interior Design: Leah Lococo Ltd. and Stephanie Krautheim
Design Layout: Patricia Escabi

T.F.H. Publications
President/CEO: Glen S. Axelrod
Executive Vice President: Mark E. Johnson
Publisher: Christopher T. Reggio
Production Manager: Kathy Bontz

T.F.H. Publications, Inc.
One TFH Plaza
Third and Union Avenues
Neptune City, NJ 07753

Discovery Communications, Inc. Book Development Team
Marjorie Kaplan, President, Animal Planet Media
Carol LeBlanc, Vice President, Licensing
Elizabeth Bakacs, Vice President, Creative Services
Brigid Ferraro, Director, Licensing
Peggy Ang, Director, Animal Planet Marketing
Caitlin Erb, Licensing Specialist

Printed and bound in China
08 09 10 11 12 1 3 5 7 9 8 6 4 2

Library of Congress Cataloging-in-Publication Data
Fernandez, Amy.
   Poodles / Amy Fernandez.
       p. cm.
   Includes index.
   ISBN 978-0-7938-3792-2 (alk. paper)
   1. Poodles. I. Title.
SF429.P85F47 2008
636.72'8—dc22
                        2007027052

This book has been published with the intent to provide accurate and authoritative information in regard to the subject matter within. While every reasonable precaution has been taken in preparation of this book, the author and publisher expressly disclaim responsibility for any errors, omissions, or adverse effects arising from the use or application of the information contained herein. The techniques and suggestions are used at the reader's discretion and are not to be considered a substitute for veterinary care. If you suspect a medical problem consult your veterinarian.

The Leader In Responsible Animal Care For Over 50 Years!®
www.tfh.com

Table of **Contents**

Chapter 1

Why I Adore My

Poodle

The Poodle is one of the most popular dog breeds in the world, especially in the United States, where he topped the charts from 1960 to 1982. No other breed has come close to breaking this record. Since then, Poodles have consistently ranked among the top ten most popular breeds in the United States. Every breed has legions of loyal fans who would never consider another type of dog, but this record constitutes an unexplainable phenomenon. What is the secret?

The Poodle's distinctive silhouette makes him one of the few universally recognizable breeds. Poodle imagery long ago infiltrated popular culture, although the trend was centuries in the making. For example, dogs sporting the characteristic Poodle clip have appeared in artwork since antiquity. In modern times, the breed has come to symbolize high style and luxury—the quintessential "blueblood" of canines.

Along with glamour, versatility is often cited as the explanation for Poodle appeal. Poodles are big and small, black and white, athletes and homebodies, and everything in between. Unlike sheepdogs or lapdogs, it's impossible to link Poodles to one particular function. In their long history, they have been hunters, athletes, war dogs, show dogs, service dogs, therapy dogs, and companions.

Every conceivable canine asset seems to be included in the Poodle package. How did this happen?

Poodle History

Poodles were developed in Europe to be hunting dogs, and their multifaceted skills made them indispensable almost immediately. Originally they were classified as water dogs. Sportsmen quickly discovered their amazing range of talents, and Poodles were soon tracking, flushing, pointing, and retrieving game on land. At the same time, they earned equally stellar status as performing dogs and stylish pets.

Origins of the Poodle

The modern Poodle can fairly be called an international effort. Developed extensively in Germany and Spain, the breed emerged as a definite type in eighteenth century France,

Notable Poodle Owners

Throughout history, Poodles have enjoyed life as companions to some of the world's greatest statesmen, artists, writers, composers, philosophers, entertainers, and athletes. A few notable Poodle lovers include Oliver Cromwell, Alexander Pope, Richard Wagner, Winston Churchill, Thomas Carlyle, Charles Dickens, Arthur Schopenhauer, Thomas Gainsborough, Edgar Allan Poe, Victor Hugo, Helen Keller, Judy Garland, Helen Hayes, Lillian Hellman, Sophia Loren, Katharine Hepburn, Zsa Zsa Gabor, Kirk Douglas, Cary Grant, Gypsy Rose Lee, Grace Kelly, Sugar Ray Robinson, James Thurber, Gertrude Stein, Liberace, John Steinbeck, Vladimir Putin, Neil Simon, Jackson Pollock, Barbara Walters, Andrew Wyeth, and Pablo Picasso.

The Poodle's elaborate haircut was developed to keep his joints warm in icy waters while hunting.

where today it has been designated as the national dog. British breeders were responsible for dramatic improvements in coat and colors found in the breed a century later.

The earliest descriptions of Poodle-type dogs place the breed's forerunners in Spain during the twelfth century, when the Moors occupied most of the Iberian Peninsula. These renowned plant and animal breeders were responsible for introducing numerous breeds of dogs, horses, and domestic livestock to Europe.

The Poodle as Hunter

Although the Poodle is valued primarily as a companion today, he was originally intended to be an improved hunting dog. In medieval times, most hunting dogs worked in packs, but new technology required dogs who were capable of working in close partnership with a single hunter. They needed to be highly responsive, sensitive, trainable, and sociable, traits that continue to define Poodle temperament.

All the Poodle's ancestors were noted for their swimming ability and skill in retrieving game from water.

Many authorities believe that the modern Poodle clip was utilitarian rather than ornamental in origin. The legs and hindquarters were shaved to ensure that the heavy coat did not impede movement while swimming. After emerging from the water, this curly hair repelled water and dried quickly, helping to warm the head, chest, and joints. In time, this functional style evolved into the modern Poodle trim.

The Poodle is believed to be closely related to the Portuguese Water Dog and Irish Water Spaniel, who also are known for their swimming ability.

The Poodle as Performer

Poodles' natural grace and agility also brought them acclaim as performing dogs. According to famed dog historian Rawdon Lee, one particularly talented troupe known as "The Ball of Little Dogs" traveled from Belgium to perform for England's Queen Anne. Because Poodles were able to perform such complicated tricks, many experts believed that they possessed larger brains than other dogs.

The Poodle as Pampered Pet

The breed also found a niche as pampered pets of royalty. In the French court of Louis XVI, the art of Poodle clipping reached its apex. Like topiary shrubs, royal pets were trimmed into bizarre geometric shapes and fancy designs. Heraldic symbols were shaved into their coats, and their huge pompadour topknots rivaled those of the court ladies.

Development of Poodle Varieties

Although Standard Poodles predominated when the breed was first introduced to Europe, three sizes—Toy, Miniature, and Standard—have been documented for centuries. All three sizes are still one breed, with no physical or temperamental differences among them.

Tiny Poodles, sometimes called "White Cubans," first became popular in France around 1850. It is theorized that this tiny size resulted from crossing Poodles, Maltese, and Toy Spaniels. However, there is no evidence that today's Toys and Minis trace back to these pets.

The Miniature was created by interbreeding smaller Standards to reduce size, while Toys were derived from small Miniatures. Miniatures and Toys began to have a consistent look only within the last 100 years or so.

The Poodle Club of America (PCA) requested separation of Standard and

The Expert Knows

Truffle Dogs

One of the Poodle's most famous jobs was truffle hunting. Toy Poodles were generally acknowledged as the premier truffle finders thanks to their intelligence and keen scenting ability. Because truffle hunting was done at night, white Poodles were preferred.

Miniature Poodles in 1931, and the AKC Board approved this change in 1932. Before World War I, Standard and Toy Poodles were classified as separate breeds. In 1943, the American Kennel Club (AKC) designated the Toy Poodle as a third variety of the same breed.

The Poodle in America

Poodles arrived in the United States from England in the late 1800s. They were first documented in the AKC's studbook in 1887. America's first Poodle club was formed in 1889 but soon disbanded because the breed was so rare at that time. Just one Poodle was AKC registered in 1890, and only 34 were registered by 1930.

The breed finally developed a following after the Poodle Club of America was formed in 1931. Forty-five were registered in 1932 and 105 in 1933. By 1950, the Poodle ranked 18th in AKC popularity. In part, this newfound popularity was due to Int. Ch. Nunsoe Duc De La Terrace, a dazzling white Standard bred in Switzerland and imported into the United States by breeder Mrs. Sherman Hoyt. His show career was marked by a string of stunning victories, including becoming the first Poodle to win Best in Show at Westminster, in 1935. Six more Poodles, representing all three sizes, have managed that feat since then. Fads and fashions have honed many breeds to one particular size, variety, or color. In contrast, the Poodle has endured in all forms, attesting to the breed's tremendous popularity.

There are three varieties of Poodle: Toy, Miniature, and Standard.

SENIOR DOG TIP

When Is a Poodle a Senior?

To some extent, size determines a Poodle's longevity. Miniatures and Toys can live 15 to 18 years and are usually considered geriatric around age 12. Standards typically live 10 to 13 years and start showing signs of age by the time they are 8 years old.

Physical Characteristics of the Breed

The following description of the Toy, Miniature, and Standard Poodles represents the "ideal" dog set forth by the AKC. However, Poodles who do not exactly fit the standard can still make wonderful pets.

Height and Weight

Aside from the obvious, there are essentially no differences among the three varieties.

- **Toy Poodles:** Toy Poodles measure 10 inches (25.4 cm) and under at the shoulder and weigh 4 to 6 pounds (1.8 to 2.7 kg).
- **Miniature Poodles:** Mini Poodles measure 10 to 15 inches (25.4 to 38.1 cm) at the shoulder and weigh 12 to 20 pounds (5.4 to 9.0 kg).
- **Standard Poodles:** Standards measure at least 15 inches (38.1 cm) at the shoulder. Typically, females are 22 to 25 inches (55.9 to 63.5 cm) tall and weigh 40 to 50 pounds (18.1 to 22.7 kg); males are 24 to 27 inches (61.1 to 68.6 cm) tall and weigh 60 to 70 pounds (27.2 to 31.8 kg).

Regardless of size, a Poodle must have the proper proportion of bone and muscle to be sturdy and athletic as well as elegant. He should never appear heavy and coarse or fragile and spindly.

Corded Poodles

The Poodle standard permits both curly and corded coats, although the latter are seldom seen today. Corded Poodles reached their height of popularity in Victorian England, but today they are a rarity.

The tendency to cord depends on the coat's texture and density. To encourage cords to form over the body, ears, and tail, the coat is kept oiled and twisted into "ropes" that can grow more than 18 inches (45.7 cm) long. Although corded coats look impressive, they require a tremendous amount of upkeep.

Head and Expression

The Poodle's head is long, lean, and breathtakingly elegant. His muzzle tapers delicately, never appearing blocky or pointed.

Eyes

His eyes are dark, oval, and wide set, creating an alert, intelligent expression. They are never large, round, protruding, or squinty and should always appear several shades darker than the coat color.

Ears

The Poodle's long ears are fan shaped and hang close to the sides of his head. They are set at eye level or lower, and the ear leather is long enough to reach the tip of the nose. They will appear much longer because of their profuse covering of fringe.

Teeth

The Poodle's teeth are set in a scissors bite, which means that the top incisors closely overlap the bottom incisors.

Coat

The Poodle's thick, curly coat is just as legendary as his keen intelligence. As a water retrieving hunter, this harsh, dense coat provided essential

A Poodle's eyes are wide and dark, giving him an alert, intelligent expression.

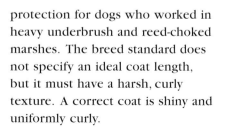

protection for dogs who worked in heavy underbrush and reed-choked marshes. The breed standard does not specify an ideal coat length, but it must have a harsh, curly texture. A correct coat is shiny and uniformly curly.

The Poodle is a versatile, friendly, and intelligent companion dog who is easy to train.

example, black Poodles are thought to be more intelligent, white Poodles more sensitive, and brown Poodles nervous and erratic. However, there is no evidence that shows that color and temperament are genetically linked.

Temperament and Behavior

The keyword of Poodle temperament is versatility. He has a balanced, easygoing nature, as well as a sense of humor that has entertained people for centuries. At the same time, the Poodle exudes a sophisticated air and is often described as stately.

Companionability

The Poodle was bred to work closely with humans and to respond readily to direction. These skills are responsible for his innate perceptiveness. His balanced disposition makes him a well-behaved house dog and an athletic outdoor companion.

This is not the breed for anyone seeking an aloof, low-key pet. Poodles are unquestionably sociable and responsive to humans thanks to centuries of selective breeding for this particular temperament. These personality traits made them superlative working dogs but also produced a legacy of loving companions.

Colors

Black and white are the traditional Poodle colors, but they are definitely not the only ones. Blues, grays, silver browns, café au laits, apricots, and creams are equally acceptable.

Common myths link particular Poodle colors to personality traits. For

Living With Poodles and Children

Poodles often head the list of breeds for families with children. However, Toy Poodles, like many fragile small breeds, are not recommended for young children. Miniatures may be the best choice; they are large enough to be sturdy but don't require a great deal of exercise and grooming.

Breeders often ask to meet a child before deciding to place a Poodle with the family. This precaution is meant to safeguard both dog and child. Children of identical ages can be quite different in personality, energy level, and maturity, which will greatly influence their ability to successfully relate to a dog.

for their cleverness. Because they are such fast learners, these dogs are consistent favorites for competitive dog sports.

Poodles have an inherent knack for understanding and remembering instructions. The ability to learn complicated skills quickly was essential for a good hunting dog. Today, Poodles are universally acknowledged as one of the easiest breeds to train.

Environment

Famed for their adaptability, Poodles thrive in a tremendous range of lifestyles, although some consideration must be made for their individual needs. For instance, in a rural environment, Toy Poodles must be protected from predatory wildlife. Standard Poodles make excellent city pets as long as owners are prepared to satisfy their exercise needs.

Exercise Requirements

A Standard Poodle should have at least 45 minutes of brisk exercise daily. A Miniature requires two 15- to 20-minute outings per day, and a Toy will do fine with a couple of 10- to 15-minute walks.

Poodles get along well with other dogs, rarely showing any inclination toward jealousy or aggression. However, a Poodle will not hesitate to jump into the role of guardian or watchdog if needed.

Intelligence and Trainability

Consistently rated as one of the world's most intelligent breeds, all three Poodle varieties are renowned

The Poodle's history and character confirm that his wonderful reputation is no mere fad or accident. These dogs rightfully can be called a canine classic design.

13

Chapter 2

The Stuff of

Everyday Life

Once you have chosen your new Poodle, it's time to prepare for his arrival. Among other things, you will need supplies. Your breeder can explain precisely what your Poodle needs (and what he doesn't), as well as where to shop for the best quality and prices. For some things like grooming tools, it is better to make a one-time purchase of high-quality items. For others, like bedding, collars, and toys, choose something relatively utilitarian and replace it often. Generally, Internet retailers offer the largest selection and the most competitive prices.

Bedding

Bedding should be durable and machine washable. Ornamentation looks nice, but it's an endless temptation for dogs to chew it up. A removable cover makes for easier cleaning, but the zipper should be covered by a seam so that your dog can't gnaw on it.

Collar

Your Poodle's collar (and leash, which is discussed later) is one of the most important supplies. Fancy collars look great, but comfort, durability, and safety are more important considerations.

Buckle Collars

Flat nylon or leather buckle collars are best. The collar should be snug enough to prevent your dog from slipping his head out but loose enough that you can slip two fingers inside when it is buckled.

Buckle collars range in width from 3/8 to 1 inch (1.0 to 2.5 cm). Toy Poodles and young puppies will need the narrowest width. If that is still too large, try a cat collar. For a Miniature Poodle, a 1/2 inch (1.3 cm) width should be fine. Standard Poodles may need a 3/4 inch (1.9 cm) wide collar.

Harnesses

Many owners prefer to use a harness rather than a collar, especially for Toys. A harness is less likely to cause discomfort if the dog pulls on his leash. A "step-in" design that does not encircle the throat is best for this purpose.

Fitting a harness is a little more complicated than estimating the fit of a collar. Measure around the widest point of the dog's chest right behind his elbows, and add 2 inches (5.1 cm). However, this method is not foolproof, because harness designs vary. Trying the harness on for fit is the best way to ensure free range of motion with no chafing. Although you may choose to leave a collar on your Poodle at all times, a harness must be removed between walks. It can cause skin irritations or mats or even permanently affect a growing puppy's gait.

Choke Collars

Choke collars are not recommended for Poodles. Sensitive and responsive, Poodles don't require the training corrections of a choke collar—and using harsh methods such as this can hamper your dog's training. Additionally, choke collars can cause neck and throat injuries in fragile Toys.

Crate

The first thing you will need is a crate or carrier to transport your dog to his new home. Plan to use this item regularly for travel and training, so good quality is definitely worth the investment.

The Expert Knows

Setting Up a Schedule

The most important tool in your training repertoire is a consistent schedule. Your Poodle relies on you for all his daily needs, and he will feel more secure knowing when to expect that you will meet them. Depending on his age, his daily schedule should include one to four specific meal times, three to ten elimination times, two daily outdoor exercise sessions, and training, socialization, grooming, and play sessions. Don't underestimate the value of play as a form of training. Poodles of every age need at least 15 minutes of interactive play daily. This facilitates bonding, trust, and communication between dog and owner.

Plastic, wire, and nylon mesh crates can be found in numerous styles.

- **Plastic:** Plastic crates are the most popular type. They come in a wide range of sizes and designs, including some folding models. They are easy to clean and provide a more den-like atmosphere, which many dogs prefer. They can be accessorized with floor grates and covers. These are the only types of crates that are airline approved.
- **Wire:** Many wire crates can be folded for storage. Some dogs prefer the open design and ample ventilation. They are the best choice

for determined chewers, who may chew through plastic crates. They are safe for car travel but not acceptable for air travel.

- **Nylon mesh:** Soft-sided mesh crates are okay for well-trained dogs in a secure environment. They are not recommended for training and are definitely not sturdy enough for travel.

Your Poodle's crate should be big enough to allow him to stand up and turn around—but no larger. An overly large crate can be especially dangerous

Licensing Your Poodle

Before acquiring your Poodle, familiarize yourself with any city ordinances pertaining to dog ownership. Obtaining a dog license usually includes showing proof of rabies vaccination and paying an annual fee. Many cities require both rabies and license tags to be displayed on dogs exercised in public parks. A license also increases the likelihood that you will be reunited with your Poodle should he become lost.

for travel. Dogs don't wear seat belts, and there is a greater risk a crated dog will be bounced around or injured if the crate is jolted or dropped. A large crate is also useless for housetraining, because it will not discourage a puppy from relieving himself in the crate. (Dogs don't like to sit in their own waste, so a smaller crate makes it impossible for them to relieve themselves in one portion and rest comfortably in another.) For a larger-size Poodle, that can mean upgrading to a larger crate as he grows.

Ex-Pen or Baby Gate

While you are browsing for crates, look for at least one exercise pen or gate to keep your Poodle confined to dog-proofed areas until he is trained and acclimated to his new home. No matter how closely you intend to supervise, you will need this. Gates of varying heights can be temporarily fitted in doorways and hallways.

An exercise pen can be used indoors or outdoors to keep your dog safely confined. If you plan to use it outdoors, make sure that it is rustproof. Ex-pens range in height from 24 to 48 inches (61.0 to 121.9 cm), and many can be modified by adding or removing side panels or floors. If your Poodle is a dedicated jumper or climber, you may need to accessorize it with a lid. This is especially important for Toys, who can be injured trying to scale the side of a high pen.

Dog Proofing Your Home

To properly socialize your Poodle, you must involve him in your daily routine. Including your Poodle in your daily activities means making your home safe for him, especially because he will find ways—most of which can get him into trouble—to satisfy his intelligence and natural curiosity.

Initially, you will need to restrict his access to parts of your home for training and safety. There is no reason for dogs to have access to potentially dangerous places like garages, garden sheds, or workshops. He should never be allowed in any room that isn't "dog proofed" to remove dangers like electric cords, toxic substances, poisonous houseplants, and valuables that you prefer not to have chewed up.

As a rule, dogs are attracted to anything bearing a strong human scent. This includes everything you handle daily, like your prescription medications, ATM cards, television remote, computer mouse, and designer boots. For Toys, floor level should be carefully inspected for hazards like wall sockets and wires. Standards need eye level temptations stowed out of reach. Placing forbidden items on the kitchen counter or dining room table may be asking for trouble. Safety measures also include installing gates to prevent falls from windows, stairwells, balconies, and decks. Poodles are attracted to water, so hot tubs, pools, and ornamental ponds must be made off limits.

Garbage cans are a perpetual source of fascination for some Poodles. Getting into the garbage can be hard to discourage once the dog hits paydirt and discovers yesterday's leftovers, so you may want to invest in a dog-proof trash can. They are more expensive but virtually impossible for even the smartest Poodle to open.

Food and Water Dishes

Ceramic or stainless steel are preferable to plastic or aluminum dishes. Aluminum dishes become pitted as repeated washing wears away their finish. Plastic dishes become nicked and scratched, making them difficult to sanitize. Dogs can also develop contact allergies to plastic dishes.

Styles with higher sides will help to keep your Poodle's ear coat out of his dishes. You also can purchase a snood to protect his ears and head coat while he eats.

Grooming Supplies

Many owners opt to have their Poodles professionally groomed. This doesn't mean that no grooming is required in between visits to the beauty shop, though. At a minimum, you will need either a slicker brush or pin brush, although pin brushes with balls on the tips of the pins are not recommended, as they can tear the coat. You also will need a Greyhound comb, a metal comb with both wide and narrow teeth; mild dog shampoo; conditioning coat spray; ear cleaning solution; and a doggy toothbrush.

Housetraining Supplies

If your Poodle puppy is not completely vaccinated or leash trained, you will need interim housetraining supplies. Choices range from litter pans to piddle pads to plain old newspaper. Have whichever you choose on hand (in abundance) before your puppy arrives, along with a generous supply of paper towels, disinfectants, enzyme odor neutralizers, and deodorizers.

Cleanliness is important, but use natural products rather than chemical cleaners if possible. Trace amounts of chemicals on bedding or floors can cause illness if a small puppy ingests them.

One particular housetraining accessory has become extremely popular in recent years: the belly band. This is a wide band of durable material, wrapped around the dog's belly and lined with an absorbent pad. Because of the resulting unpleasant sensation, most dogs quickly learn to refrain from urinating while wearing one. A similar pantie-type garment is also available for female dogs. It is especially useful for dogs addicted to territorial marking or elderly dogs with incontinence problems.

Identification

Accessorize your Poodle's collar with an identification tag bearing your name and telephone number. This is the best insurance that he will be found and returned quickly if lost. If you can't find one small enough for our Toy Poodle, paint this

Dog Walkers and Doggy Day Care

In this day and age, the majority of dogs belong to working owners. You may feel guilty about the prospect of abandoning your Poodle for an 8- to 10-hour stretch, but there is no reason to forgo the pleasure of coming home to a dog after a long, hard day at work.

There are a multitude of options to ensure that your Poodle is not lonely, bored, or neglected during the workday. Professional dog walkers and doggy day care are the most common. Dog walkers range from local teenagers or seniors to full-time professionals. Likewise, day care programs range from supplemental services offered by vets and groomers to fully staffed deluxe facilities.

Your choice should be based on what you and your Poodle are comfortable with. He may not need swimming lessons or grilled salmon snacks, but he should be guaranteed consistent professional attention. Day care programs should be adequately staffed to ensure every dog's welfare and safety. Dog walkers should arrive reliably at the same time daily. This is especially important if your Poodle requires midday feeding or medication, or if your puppy is learning a housetraining schedule.

Investigate thoroughly before making a final decision. Ask for background information, get references, and talk to other owners presently using the service. Visit the day care facility, or accompany the dog walker on her rounds before entrusting her with your pet.

FAMILY-FRIENDLY TIP

How Much Should Your Child Care for the Dog?

Poodles and children are a time-honored combination, and your child will probably be absolutely thrilled when the new Poodle arrives on the scene. She will want to take part in every aspect of the dog's care. This can be an excellent learning experience, but don't overestimate a child's ability to handle these responsibilities. Even many adults have trouble learning and sticking to a dog care routine. A child's promise to take responsibility for the dog's care may be totally sincere, but be prepared to offer reminders, assistance, and constant supervision to ensure the best results for both of them.

lost and is found, a special scanner can detect the chip. Microchip identification typically lasts a lifetime. Ask your vet to scan the chip as part of your Poodle's annual checkup to ensure that it is still in place.

Leash

Your Poodle's leash should be 3/8 to 1 inch (1.0 to 2.5 cm) wide, depending on his size and strength. Many town ordinances limit the length of dog leashes to 6 feet (1.8 m). That is not the only reason why long leashes are not recommended; it is also much harder to safeguard a dog on a long leash. Retractable flex leashes are fine in protected quiet areas. On busy streets, an active dog on a flex lead can easily run into oncoming traffic or trip a pedestrian.

Canvas, nylon, and leather leads are fine for Poodles. Your choice depends on taste, comfort, and price range, but a heavier material is best for very strong

information on his collar with fabric paint.

A microchip is another form of identification that you may want to consider. Implanting a microchip is a safe, relatively painless procedure similar to a vaccination. The chip bears a unique number that you must register with the appropriate agency; if your dog becomes

Proper identification is essential for your Poodle in the event that he ever becomes lost.

Poodles. Expensive leather designer leads may not be the best choice for puppies addicted to chewing.

Make sure that the leash you choose has a sturdy clip. Inferior designs can break or open if your dog pulls hard enough. This can be fatal in high-traffic areas.

Pet Stroller

A pet stroller is handy when traveling with Toys and puppies on busy streets. It's also useful if you're traveling with your Toy or a puppy via public transportation.

Toys and Chews

Your Poodle needs a nice assortment of toys and safe chews. When selecting these, keep in mind that there are no federal safety standards for pet toys, so you must rely on careful judgment and your breeder's advice. Never assume that every toy for sale is safe for your Poodle.

Baby toys can be a safe alternative for Toys and young puppies. For Miniature and Standard Poodles, stick with large hard rubber balls, stuffable chew toys, knotted ropes, and nylon bones. Dental chews should only be given under supervision.

As a rule Poodle care is easy, but choosing the proper equipment plays a big part in this. A bit of care and planning can ensure that life with your Poodle is every bit as delightful as you envisioned.

SENIOR DOG TIP

Helping Your Senior Adapt

Potential owners sometimes worry that older dogs won't adjust to a new home. This is an unfortunate misconception. Older Poodles often adapt more readily than puppies to a new home because they are already socialized and trained. Of course, even the most easygoing Poodle needs time to adapt to major changes in his life.

When he first arrives, conform to his previous routine as much as possible. Don't abruptly change his diet, and gradually accustom him to your local tap water by mixing it with bottled water for the first week. Implement a housetraining schedule even if he is already trained. He cannot be expected to know when or where he should eliminate unless you clearly and consistently communicate the rules.

If you plan to exercise your Poodle in a fenced yard, supervise carefully to make sure that he cannot jump over or dig under the fence. And don't overwhelm him with too many introductions to other pets, neighbors, and friends at first.

Chapter 3

Good Eating

It's hard to believe that commercial dog food didn't become widely available until after World War II. In addition to the thousands of foods on the market, dog owners now can select from countless supplements, treats, doggy drinks, desserts, and special diets to enhance their pets' daily fare. It makes you wonder how dogs survived and thrived without any of these items until 50 years ago. There are a couple of reasons to explain this.

eft to their own devices, as most dogs were in the past, they found and ate a wide variety of foods every day. Not all of it was equally wholesome, but variety guaranteed balance. It is also important to realize that canine nutrition was a poorly understood science until recent decades. Modern research has answered many questions about what our dogs require (and don't require) in a balanced diet. This plethora of information has inevitably spawned its own share of misunderstanding, dietary fads, contradictory experts, and urban legends about dog food.

Your dog's dietary needs will change throughout his life based on his age, activity level, and overall health.

In the face of this information overload, it seems nearly impossible to properly choose the right diet for your Poodle. The good news is that it doesn't need to be complicated. Common sense and your dog's physical condition should be your guide. Your Poodle's dietary needs will change throughout his life, but there are complete, balanced diets designed for puppies, adults, and seniors. Proper body weight, muscle tone, healthy skin and coat, and a good appetite are adequate proof that his diet is nutritious.

How to Feed a Balanced Diet

Regardless of age or size, every Poodle must have a diet that contains a proper balance of proteins, carbohydrates, fats, vitamins, and minerals. The easiest way to ensure this is by feeding an Association of American Feed Control Officials (AAFCO) guaranteed premium commercial food. Better yet, the label should state that this assessment was verified through strictly controlled feeding trials.

Examine Feeding Instructions

The feeding instructions on dog food labels are broadly calculated based on breed, age, and size; the recommended portions tend to be extremely generous. Your Poodle's weight, condition, activity level, and metabolism are equally important considerations when estimating portion size for his needs. A large Standard Poodle spending his days hunting may need generous portions of a premium formula high in fat and protein, for example. A tiny Toy Poodle spending his days on the settee will have very different requirements.

Inspect Ingredients

AAFCO labeling requires ingredients to be listed in descending order based on their relative percentage by weight. The top ingredients should be protein from meat sources rather than cereal. Although every dog needs some fat and protein in his diet, the percentages of fat and protein vary greatly in different brands. Canned foods may contain from 8 to 15 percent protein and 2 to 15 percent fat. Dry foods can contain 18 to 30 percent protein and 5 to 20 percent fat. More is not necessarily better.

Review the Guaranteed Analysis

An AAFCO endorsement doesn't automatically mean that every food labeled as such is equally good for every Poodle. The guaranteed analysis on the label merely states the minimum amount of fat and protein and the maximum amount of crude fiber, ash, and moisture that is present in the food. These ingredients can come from many sources with varying nutritional value.

Dogs are omnivorous; they can digest a wide range of foods. This ability was crucial to the species' survival. However, their digestive system is designed to most efficiently utilize

Table Manners

Polite table manners don't come naturally to most dogs. From puppyhood, they learn to eat in a highly competitive situation where bad manners rule the day. It is your responsibility to teach your Poodle acceptable mealtime behavior. If he gets into the habit of barking and jumping to demand his food, begs at the table, or grabs food off your plate, you have only yourself to blame. Food is a tremendous motivator, and your dog will quickly learn better manners if you consistently discourage bad habits and reward good ones. Tell him to sit quietly while you prepare his food, and do not give him his dish until he cooperates. (To learn how to teach the *sit* command, see Chapter 6.)

Part of your Poodle's table manners includes teaching him never to growl or snap while eating. The first signs of this behavior must be reprimanded immediately. He should never object to being approached or touched while eating, and he should always permit you to take something out of his mouth. That does not mean it's okay for a child to tease your Poodle while he is eating. This is one of the most common scenarios leading to dog bites.

Keep a close eye on the ingredients in your dog's food; avoid foods containing meat or grain by-products.

except that by-products, typically found in canned food, are not heat processed.

Likewise, carbohydrates can come from many different sources, most commonly rice, wheat, and corn. A balanced canine diet must include some carbohydrates, but foods comprising primarily grain are not nutritionally adequate for dogs. Whole grains are preferable to grain by-products. Many breeders prefer to avoid foods that contain soy or wheat because both are common triggers of food allergies. In addition, wheat gluten has been identified as the source in some contaminated pet food recalls.

Careful scrutiny of the label is especially important when selecting a natural food. We are familiar with the requirements for organic food labeling of products destined for human consumption (no antibiotics, no pesticides, no synthetic ingredients). But these same standards do not apply to dog food. Statements like "natural, human grade, veterinarian approved, or healthy" are not official terms subject to any regulation or verification. Check the source of ingredients to ensure the truth of these claims.

meat. This should be the primary ingredient in your Poodle's diet. Meat proteins can come from meat, meat by-products, or meat meal—all very different things. Avoid foods containing meal and meat by-products, which are derived from skin, organs, fatty tissue, feet, and heads. Meal and meat by-products are essentially the same

Commercial Foods

Commercial foods contain varying amounts of additives approved by the Food and Drug Administration (FDA),

The following sample charts provide feeding guidelines for Toy, Miniature, and Standard Poodles. Please keep in mind that they are guidelines only; consult your veterinarian for recommendations tailored to your dog's specific needs.

Toy Poodle

	Puppies (2 to 6 months)	Adolescents (6 to 18 months)	Active Adults (18 months to 10 years)	Sedentary Adults (18 months to 10 years)	Seniors (10 years and older)
Times per Day	4 times	3 times	3 times	2 times	2 times
Amount	1/2 cup (118.3 ml) per meal	3/4 cup (177.4 ml) per meal	1/2 cup (118.3 ml) per meal	1/2 cup (118.3 ml) per meal	1/2 cup (118.3 ml) per meal
Best Food	growth formula	growth formula	adult toy breed/maintenance	adult toy breed/maintenance	senior or growth formula

Miniature Poodle

	Puppies (2 to 6 months)	Adolescents (6 to 18 months)	Active Adults (18 months to 8 years)	Sedentary Adults (18 months to 8 years)	Seniors (8 years and older)
Times per Day	4 times	3 times	2 times	2 times	2 times
Amount	1/2 cup (236.6 ml) per meal	3/4 cup (236.6 ml) per meal	1 cup (236.6 ml) per meal	3/4 cup (177.4 ml) per meal	3/4 cup (177.4 ml) per meal
Best Food	growth formula	growth formula	adult maintenance formula	adult maintenance formula	senior formula

Standard Poodle

	Puppies (2 to 6 months)	Adolescents (6 to 18 months)	Active Adults (18 months to 7 years)	Sedentary Adults (18 months to 7 years)	Seniors (7 years and older)
Times per Day	4 times	3 times	3 times	3 times	3 times
Amount	1 1/2 to 2 cups (354.9 to 473.2 ml) per meal	2 cups (473.2 ml) per meal	2 cups (473.2 ml) per meal	1 1/2 cups (354.9 ml) per meal	1 1/2 cups (354.9 ml) per meal
Best Food	large breed growth formula	large breed growth formula	adult maintenance or performance formula for large breeds	adult maintenance formula for large breeds	senior formula

FAMILY-FRIENDLY TIP

Children and Feeding the Family Dog

More and more studies confirm the psychological benefits of consistent mealtime routines. Involving your child in your daily routine to feed the dog can have the same satisfying effects. However, giving a young child sole responsibility for this can be a recipe for trouble. Ultimately, an adult must be willing to supervise all aspects of a dog's daily routine. In addition to possibly forgetting to feed the dog, a child might inadvertently overfeed or underfeed without noticing the accumulating consequences. A young child might be asked to help you prepare the dog's food, make sure his water bowl is always full, or remind you when he has finished his dinner.

like synthetic vitamins and minerals, natural and chemical preservatives, and artificial ingredients to enhance color, flavor, and texture. Plenty of highly processed foods containing these additives are also available on the shelves of the local grocery store. We commonly refer to foods with these additives as "junk food" because they are not the healthiest choice for your Poodle. Commercial foods do not invariably contain artificial ingredients, though. There are healthy choices available, but you must evaluate the ingredient lists, rather than dog food advertisements, to find them.

Breeders recommend a wide range of canned, dry, and frozen commercial foods, and Poodles can thrive on any of these. Your choice should be based on the quality of ingredients and your Poodle's resultant health and condition.

Dry

Dry food, or kibble, is the most popular type of dog food. It is relatively inexpensive, easy to store, and convenient to feed. Companies invest a lot of money researching canine nutritional needs and taste preferences. As a result, well-known premium brands are consistently reliable in content, formula, and palatability.

In recent years, some manufacturers have introduced formulas tailored for large and small dogs, and even specific breeds. In addition to variations in the content, the size of the kibble is customized to make it more appealing to puppies, adults, and large and small dogs. Kibble's crunchy texture also aids in tartar control by helping to keep plaque from accumulating on tooth surfaces and by reducing calcium levels in saliva, a major component of dental plaque.

On the other hand, some kibbles may contain up to 60 percent starch, inferior sources of protein, and chemical preservatives, so it is important to check out the fine print on the label and avoid generic brands. Dry food will remain fresh for approximately three months after being opened, because preservatives are added to prevent the fat-based ingredients from becoming rancid. Synthetic preservatives such as butylated hydroxyanisole (BHA), butylated hydroxytoluene (BHT), and ethoxyquin are FDA approved, but they remain controversial. Some brands are naturally preserved with vitamin E or C, but these will have a shorter shelf life.

Canned

The advantages of canned food are variety, taste appeal, a long shelf life, and fewer artificial ingredients. The food is sterilized and heat sealed in the can, preserving it until it's opened.

In general, canned foods contain between 8 percent and 15 percent protein and 2 percent and 15 percent fat, but a dog must consume relatively more canned food, which is approximately 75 percent water, than dry to meet the same nutritional requirements. This is one of the reasons why few breeders and vets advocate feeding canned food exclusively. Canned food will not contribute to dental hygiene, and many dogs prefer foods with a more challenging texture. You can compromise by mixing a small amount of canned food with kibble to get the combined benefits of taste appeal and hard texture. Add just enough to flavor the food without softening its texture too much.

Dry food, or kibble, is the most popular type of commercial diet.

Semi-Moist

Although they are convenient, most breeders do not recommend semi-moist foods because they contain large amounts of starch, sugar, artificial dyes, preservatives, and synthetic flavorings. They are produced to resemble chunks of meat or ground beef, but their appearance is deceptive. They may be chewy and tasty, but they usually comprise low-quality ingredients. Semi-moist foods are not especially nutritious, will not help to prevent plaque formation, and can be a major source of allergy problems.

Noncommercial Diets

Preparing a noncommercial food for your Poodle is the only way to strictly control what he eats. Two common noncommercial diets are home cooked and raw.

Home-Cooked Diets

Home-cooked diets have gained popularity as consumers became more aware of potentially unhealthy ingredients in many prepackaged foods. When you cook for yourself, you have the option of forgoing processed convenience foods in favor of fresh ingredients, and there is no reason why you cannot do the same for your

Poodle. Home cooking also may be necessary for Poodles who are suffering from various allergies or digestive problems.

However, the last thing you want to do is create nutritional problems when trying to improve your dog's diet. This is not the place for experimentation or shortcuts. Giving your Poodle a share of your dinner does not constitute a balanced home-cooked diet. His diet must contain a variety of meats, grains, and vegetables. Dogs digest meat very efficiently, but grain and vegetable ingredients must be cooked thoroughly for dogs to completely digest them. Many nutritionists also recommend giving vitamin/mineral supplements when feeding

You can strictly control what your Poodle eats with a noncommercial diet.

homemade diets. Consult with your vet or a canine nutritionist, and do your own research before designing a meal plan for your dog.

Raw Diets

A raw meat diet, commonly known as the BARF (bones and raw food) diet, has become the most popular natural dietary alternative. This diet aims to recreate the ancestral canine diet— primarily live game—which is obviously difficult for most dog owners to procure on a daily basis. The modern-day version consists mainly of raw chicken, usually the less expensive backs and necks, supplemented with raw meat, bones, eggs, fruits, and vegetables.

Most dogs will happily consume the raw meat, poultry, and bones, but some are less keen to accept the fruits and vegetables, which can lead to dietary imbalance. Feeding a raw diet is also very messy. You will need to disinfect all surfaces that come in contact with the raw meat. This could mean mopping the kitchen floor and washing your Poodle's crate every day. Your Poodle also will need more frequent bathing to remove stains and meat juices from his coat. Additionally, keep in mind that Miniature and Standard Poodles may have the jaw power to tackle bones and large chunks of meat, but Toy Poodles may not. You may have to cut their meat into small pieces to prevent choking. And finally, the potential risks of undercooked or raw meat, like salmonellosis and E. coli infection, apply equally to dogs. Cooking is the most effective way to neutralize pathogens.

Canine health professionals ranging from vets to breeders to behaviorists have endorsed the BARF diet. Advocates claim that it can cure or prevent a vast array of health and problem behaviors. Many of these claims are valid, but common sense should prevail when deciding whether this is the best choice for your Poodle. Talk to your vet and your Poodle's breeder, and do some independent research.

Supplements

Your Poodle does not need dietary supplements if he is fed a complete, balanced diet. At best they are unnecessary and in some cases may actually be harmful. The fact that vitamins and herbal supplements are sold in health food stores doesn't guarantee complete safety. Nor does it mean that if a little is good, a lot is better.

Excessive doses of some minerals and vitamins will simply be excreted, but that is not true of all of them. Vitamins A and C, calcium, and selenium, to name a few, can build up to toxic levels and damage major organs. Some also can adversely react with prescription medications or neutralize their effectiveness.

If your breeder or veterinarian recommends supplements for your Poodle, stick with brands made specifically for dogs that bear either CL (Consumer Lab) or USP (United States Pharmacopoeia) guarantees. These endorsements are your best protection against false labeling and impure ingredients.

Water

Clean, fresh water is a crucial ingredient in any healthy diet. If you normally don't drink your tap water, don't give it to your Poodle, either. Local water with a high mineral content can exacerbate

tearstaining problems, and some dogs can develop digestive upsets from unfamiliar tap water.

If your Poodle puppy came from a commercial breeder or pet shop, make sure that he can drink from a dish. Dogs in commercial kennels normally don't have water bowls— they only have feeder-type bottles to drink from. A small puppy can become seriously dehydrated before he learns how to lap water from a dish.

If you want to encourage your Poodle to drink more water during hot weather or heavy exercise, try offering clear chicken broth, flavored ice cubes, or designer dog drinks to tempt him. Designer drinks are similar to the vitamin waters and flavored waters that have become popular for human consumption. They can be purchased at specialty pet food shops. Before you buy any of these products, check the ingredients for chemical preservatives and artificial coloring, which may cause facial staining or allergies.

Free Feeding Versus Scheduled Feeding

Leaving food available for your Poodle at all times is certainly convenient. You don't have to worry about rushing home to fix his dinner. And you have the comfort of knowing that he can simply help himself when he is hungry. Despite these advantages, breeders generally avoid the practice of free feeding.

For one thing, only dry foods can be safely left at room temperature for several hours. Also, free feeding does not usually prove to be a workable system for multi-dog households, the reason being that there is there no way to guarantee that every dog gets a fair share of the food. Food is also one of the most common triggers for possessiveness and rivalry, so dogs may be encouraged to overeat in a competitive situation or become intimidated into not eating at all. The biggest drawback to free feeding is that lack of supervision makes it difficult to notice whether your Poodle has gone off his food. Lack of appetite is often the earliest warning sign of a budding health problem.

Scheduled feeding is the best way to help your Poodle develop good eating habits, learn polite manners, and maintain his ideal weight. Feed him in the same place at the same time every day. Pick up his dish after approximately 20 minutes, regardless of whether he has finished. Even if he picks at his dish, begs, or demands seconds, don't offer him anything else until his next mealtime. He will not be encouraged to try these stunts if he knows he won't be fed again until his next scheduled mealtime.

SENIOR DOG TIP

Feeding the Older Dog

Geriatric Poodles may need dietary revisions for many reasons, but the mere fact of reaching a certain age is not one of them. Consult your vet before changing your Poodle's diet. Older dogs have lower energy requirements and may need fewer calories, but their diet still must include adequate nutrients and sufficient protein to maintain muscle mass. On the other hand, certain age-related health problems may warrant a low-fat or low-protein diet. Senior dog formulas contain approximately 27 percent protein and 12 percent fat. Elderly dogs may also do better with smaller-sized kibble, softer foods, and smaller, more frequent meals.

If your senior Poodle's normal appetite suddenly changes, don't take a wait-and-see approach. Weakness, pain, mental confusion, or tooth decay can undermine a senior dog's normal appetite, and some metabolic disorders can drastically increase his appetite. Biannual checkups may reveal early indications of health problems that can be controlled or minimized through diet.

To prevent obesity, monitor your Poodle's diet and make sure that he gets enough exercise.

Obesity

Owners often agonize about whether their dog is eating enough or consuming a balanced diet. Ironically, obesity is by far the most prevalent nutritional problem affecting America's dogs. This serious condition increases a dog's risk for heart and liver disease, pancreatitis, diabetes, arthritis, and bladder cancer.

Why Are so Many Dogs Overweight?

You must exercise self-control for your Poodle. Although commercial dog food may contain up to 2,000 calories per 1 pound (0.5 kg) of food, it is rarely the reason why Poodles become overweight. The obesity epidemic is a result of overindulging in foods, especially treats and table scraps.

Treats

Treats should never compose more than 10 percent of your Poodle's daily food intake, and they should be chosen as carefully as his regular food. Many of them are chock-full of fat, sugar, and artificial ingredients. Dog treats are not required to meet any AAFCO nutritional standards, but all ingredients must appear on the label. Poodles are smart, but until they start doing their own grocery shopping, it is your job to select brands that are low in fat and that have natural ingredients. If your Poodle is slightly overweight, skip the dog treats and substitute low-fat cheese cubes, bits of fruit, vegetable snacks like carrot sticks, and unsweetened cereal.

Switching to low-cal treats won't help if your Poodle is already seriously overweight. You should be able to feel his ribs, and he should have some indication of a waistline. If he has a layer of fat around his chest, middle, or back, it is time to cut down on treats.

Table Scraps

Human food, per se, is not necessarily bad for dogs. The problem is the wide range of foods we normally eat. Reasonable quantities of foods like lean meats and cooked vegetables are not going to harm your Poodle any more than they harm you. However, it's normal for dogs to develop a taste for things like lamb chops, which can cause picky eating habits. Your Poodle will soon realize that refusing his dog food means that grilled salmon is probably on the way. If this becomes a daily pattern, it will lead to nutritional imbalances because canines and humans have quite different requirements. Also, dogs love many human foods that are not good for them, such as pizza, ice cream, and five-alarm chili. Inadvisable choices like these can cause devastating digestive problems in Poodles.

If you get into the habit of sharing every meal with your Poodle, he will likely develop vitamin deficiencies and poor eating habits in addition to indigestion and obesity.

Preventing Bloat in Standard Poodles

Gastric torsion, commonly known as bloat, can strike any large deep-chested dog. Although physical structure and genetics play a role, this life-threatening condition is triggered by the sudden buildup of gas and fluids in a dog's digestive tract. Feeding practices can help to minimize the risk of this occurrence. Divide your Standard Poodle's daily rations into two or more small meals rather than offering him one large serving per day. Avoid commercial foods containing citric acid preservatives. Pre-moisten kibble by mixing it with canned food or broth before serving. Also, do not use raised bowls when feeding.

"Lite" Dog Foods

An indicator of how prevalent obesity has become is the multitude of "lite" dog foods on the market. There are no AAFCO guidelines for diet dog foods, but the label must state how much lower in fat or calories the product is compared to the company's regular formula. The maximum caloric AAFCO allowances for light foods are 1,409 calories per 1 pound (0.5 kg) for kibble and 409 calories per 1 pound (0.5 kg) for canned, which is not all that low. Feeding your Poodle a lite food will not make much of a difference unless you also limit his portion size and cut out the junk food. Many lite foods contain high levels of fiber to make them more filling. This will result in noticeably more yard cleanup and can possibly lead to nutritional deficiencies in Toy Poodles.

Choosing the perfect diet for your Poodle can seem over-whelming, but there are many acceptable options that will ensure that he eats a healthy, balanced diet. Never underestimate how important this is!

Chapter 4

Looking Good

Mention dog grooming, and Poodles are the first breed that comes to mind. A perfectly coifed Poodle is indeed a breathtaking sight, often considered the apex of a groomer's skills.

Whether you intend to keep your Poodle in a show coat or a utilitarian clip, he needs regular grooming. You can do this yourself, or you can seek the services of a professional. Be realistic about how much grooming you are willing and able to manage and how much money you are prepared to spend for professional grooming.

Poodle grooming is not exactly rocket science, but it does require a fair degree of skill and artistic sense. Plenty of practice and the proper tools are essential. Grooming guides available in a multitude of formats can help you get started, but you also should attend a grooming course or get hands-on demonstrations from a breeder before attempting the job on your own. This chapter will give you a general idea of how to handle all aspects of your Poodle's grooming routine.

Grooming Supplies

Poodle grooming supplies can range from a few basics to a full set of top-of-the-line equipment. Although it will save you a fortune in professional grooming, the initial outlay can be substantial. You will need:

- comb and brush: metal comb with coarse teeth, pin brush with long pins and no balls on the tips of the pins, slicker brush
- cordless clipper with blades for varying coat lengths
- cotton balls
- detangling spray
- doggy shampoo and conditioner
- doggy toothbrush and toothpaste
- ear-cleaning solution
- free-standing dryer
- good-quality scissors
- guillotine-style nail clippers
- nail file
- professional-quality grooming table
- styptic powder
- towels

Grooming as Health Check

Your Poodle's grooming session is the perfect opportunity to give him a quick health check. By doing this regularly, you will be thoroughly familiar with his normal health and quick to spot anything out of the ordinary. Run your hands over his body, searching for any unusual lumps, injuries, or tender spots. Examine his coat for ticks, flea dirt, and skin irritations. His weight and muscle tone should remain fairly stable. Check his eyes for any signs of redness, squinting, hazing, or tearing. They should be bright, shiny, and dark. His expression should be calm and alert. You should not notice any strong odor coming from his ears or mouth. His ear leather and gums should be pale pink, with no signs of swelling or tenderness. Most of all, he should not show any reluctance to be examined. Sudden shyness, crankiness, or lethargy can signal early signs of illness.

Brushing

Poodles don't shed much, which sometimes gives the erroneous impression that they don't need brushing. Their coats are fast growing and prone to tangling if dead hair is allowed to accumulate for any length of time. A neglected Poodle coat will quickly evolve into a nightmarish mix of dead hair, dirt, and impenetrable mats. Daily brushing is preferable, but a minimum of two or three thorough brushings a week are mandatory. Needless to say, grooming smaller Toy and Mini Poodles will require relatively less time and effort than brushing the coat of a Standard.

Poodle experts can debate the merits of various brushes endlessly, but both slicker brushes and pin brushes can be used. Your choice ultimately depends on the texture and density of your Poodle's coat. Slicker brushes are excellent at getting through dense parts of the coat and removing mats. They are made up of flexible wires that are short, closely spaced, thin, and flexible; the wires are set into a flat rectangular base. A pin brush is made of long, straight pins set into a rubber cushion. A pin brush is gentler on the coat but will not penetrate a dense coat as easily. It works best for longer parts of the coat, such as ear fringe and topknots.

How to Brush Your Poodle

Begin by brushing the hindquarters, and then move on to the legs, body, and neck using short up-and-down strokes. Be sure that the brush penetrates completely through the coat, but do not allow it to rake the skin, which can cause a painful brush burn.

Pay careful attention to the abdomen and chest, especially under the front legs, prime areas where mats form. If you find a mat, pull it apart with

Whether you keep your Poodle in a show coat, like this one, or a pet clip, regular grooming will be a necessity.

your fingers, alternately brushing it apart with a small slicker brush while saturating it with detangling spray. Brush the head and ears last, gently using a pin brush. After the coat is

41

A Poodle requires frequent brushing—as often as once a day—to prevent painful mats from forming in his coat.

dog shampoos and conditioners on the market designed to do everything from deodorizing, moisturizing, color enhancing texturizing, and detangling. If you are not sure what to use, ask your breeder or groomer. Avoid any harsh products that may dry the coat or skin. Very sudsy shampoos can leave a soapy residue, and conditioners containing wax may impart a nice shine but can cause coat damage as they build up.

How to Bathe Your Poodle

Toys and Minis can be bathed in a kitchen sink or laundry tub. For a Standard, you will need a full-sized bathtub. Place a nonskid mat in the bottom of the tub or sink, and attach a bath tether to prevent the dog from jumping out. Next, wet your entire dog with warm water. The Poodle's coat is designed to repel water, so be thorough. Massage the shampoo in all the way to the skin, working from head to tail. Some groomers prefer using a large sponge or bath brush for this. Keep his head tilted upward to avoid getting soap in his eyes or water in the ears. Pay special attention to his feet, legs, and the base of his tail.

Then, rinse well and reapply shampoo. Use a spray attachment for rinsing. You won't be able to completely rinse out the soap by just pouring water over your dog. If you

thoroughly brushed, comb through it all the way to the skin to make sure that you have not missed any small mats.

Bathing

Normally, a bath every six to eight weeks will keep your Poodle looking smart. Spot-cleaning his feet and face with pre-moistened doggy wipes helps to keep him presentable between baths, although more frequent bathing may be needed if he spends a lot of time outdoors.

Your Poodle must be completely brushed prior to bathing—removing mats becomes a far worse job after the coat is wet. There are a multitude of notice your Poodle scratching after a bath, soap residue may be irritating his skin.

The Poodle's coat must be conditioned after each bath to keep the coat ends from drying. A leave-in conditioner won't work for this. Leave the conditioner in for a few minutes before the final rinse.

Before removing your dog from the tub, gently squeeze excess water from his coat, blot him dry as much as possible, get out of the way, and let him have a good shake.

How to Dry Your Poodle

Left to air dry, your Poodle's coat will form into coarse, tight ringlets. A dryer is the best way to prevent chilling and create a lovely fluffy look. You will need both hands free to simultaneously brush and dry, so a stand dryer is recommended. Set it on low/warm, and test it on your skin before turning it on your dog. Never set it on high or leave an unattended dog under a dryer.

Use a pin and/or slicker brush to simultaneously brush and dry your dog's coat one section at a time. Point the dryer at one small section, and brush quickly until it is dry. Begin with the topknot and ears, using your pin brush. Be sure to remove any traces of moisture that may have accumulated in his ears after the bath; dampness can lead to yeast infections. When his head is dry, move on to the neck, chest, and front legs, fluffing with the slicker brush. Next, do the back, tail, rump, back legs, and abdomen.

The Expert Knows

The Grooming Table

A grooming table isn't essential, but it can make many aspects of your Poodle's routine care easier. It places him at eye level and gives him a firm footing. A grooming arm and noose attached to the corner can provide additional security if needed.

Select a sturdy model, large enough to give him plenty of standing room, with ribbing running across the width of the table rather than lengthwise. Needless to say, a table will do no good unless you take the time to table train your Poodle. He should be placed on the table daily until he can be relied on to remain there calmly without fidgeting or trying to jump off. Praise and tidbits should be a part of his table experience as much as nail trimming to foster a positive association.

After shampooing your Poodle, rinse him thoroughly.

Keeping the wet portions of your Poodle's coat covered by a towel prevents him from becoming chilled and keeps the coat from curling. If the coat begins to dry before you are finished, dampen it with a sprayer and continue drying.

Clipping the Coat

The custom of clipping Poodles has been documented in art and literature for centuries. A multitude of fanciful styles have come and gone, but the "Lion Clip" remains universally associated with the breed. According to legend, this pattern evolved to permit a water dog unrestrained movement when swimming while protecting his chest and joints. It's questionable how much warmth and protection a soaking-wet coat could provide, but this style eventually evolved into the Continental Clip seen in the show ring today.

Today, all acceptable trims permit the head coat, known as the topknot, to be tied back with elastic bands. The custom of tying the Poodle's topknot with a ribbon served two purposes. It ensured unobstructed vision when hunting, and more importantly, brightly colored ribbons helped hunters recognize their dogs and differentiate them from quarry. This was crucial when black was the predominant Poodle color.

Four trims are allowed by the Poodle breed standard today: the Continental Clip, English Saddle Clip, Sporting Clip, and Puppy Clip. These are the official trims permitted for Poodles in the show ring but are far from the only ones. Comfort and creativity can be combined in infinite ways to enhance your Poodle's beauty. Dog groomers usually have their own favorite Poodle trims, and these can be modified to suit individual preferences.

Continental Clip

The Continental Clip is the most common Poodle trim. The face, throat, feet, and base of the tail are shaved. The hindquarters are shaved except for two pompons, known as rosettes, on the hips. The legs are shaved, leaving bracelets over the hocks and puffs at the pastern joints on the forelegs. A rounded pompon is left at the tail tip. The topknot is long and held off the face with a series of elastic bands. Unclipped portions of the coat can be left 2¹/2 to 3 inches (6.4 to 7.6 cm) long and shaped with scissors to enhance the Poodle's proportions.

English Saddle Clip

In the English Saddle Clip, the face, throat, base of the tail, and feet are shaved. The forelegs are shaved, leaving puffs at the pasterns. A rounded pompon is left at the tail tip. The coat on the hindquarters is trimmed short, with two curved areas shaved onto the flanks. Two bands are shaved onto each hind leg. The rest of the coat is left full and shaped to the body's outline.

Sporting Clip

In the Sporting Clip, the face, feet, throat, and base of the tail are shaved. The topknot is scissored into a cap on the head, and a pompon is formed on the tail. The coat on the body and legs is clipped or scissored to follow the body's contour. The coat should not be more than 1 inch (2.5 cm) long, although the coat on the legs may be slightly longer.

Puppy Clip

Poodles less than a year old are customarily shown in a Puppy Clip. In

this clip, the face, throat, feet, and base of the tail are shaved. The pompon on the tail and the coat on the body are shaped with scissors.

Nail and Foot Care

Your Poodle's feet and nails should be frequently checked for injuries, broken nails, or debris between the toe pads. He may need his nails trimmed every two to four weeks. If his nails touch the floor and "click" when he walks, they need a trim. Your dog's feet can become permanently damaged from walking on overgrown nails.

Many dogs are sensitive about having their feet handled, but it's an

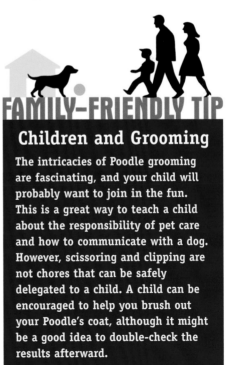

FAMILY-FRIENDLY TIP
Children and Grooming

The intricacies of Poodle grooming are fascinating, and your child will probably want to join in the fun. This is a great way to teach a child about the responsibility of pet care and how to communicate with a dog. However, scissoring and clipping are not chores that can be safely delegated to a child. A child can be encouraged to help you brush out your Poodle's coat, although it might be a good idea to double-check the results afterward.

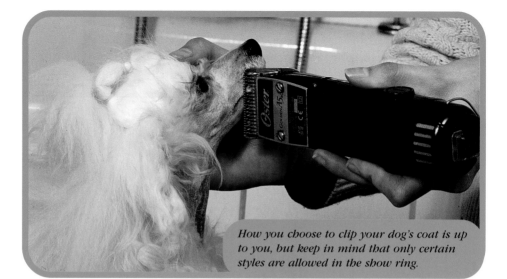

How you choose to clip your dog's coat is up to you, but keep in mind that only certain styles are allowed in the show ring.

essential part of the grooming process. Begin teaching your Poodle to accept having his nails trimmed and feet shaved as soon as you get him. Be persistent, but don't lose your temper or turn it into a confrontation. If he becomes upset, stop. Always praise him when he cooperates, and do it every day until he overcomes his reluctance.

How to Trim Your Poodle's Nails

To trim your dog's nails, you will need guillotine-style nail clippers, styptic powder (to stop bleeding in case you cut the nail too far), and a nail file.

Stand your Poodle on a table, or hold him on your lap. Hold his paw firmly in one hand, with your thumb over the top of the paw and fingers underneath to slightly spread his toes apart. Hook the tip of the nail into the clipper blade, and squeeze quickly and firmly. Make sure that the blade in the clipper is sharp; a dull blade can make a painful, ragged cut. Use your file to smooth down the nail edges after clipping.

Trimming your Poodle's nails regularly is the best insurance against accidentally cutting into the quick, the tiny vein running through the nail. Trim away only the portion extending past the quick a little bit at a time. If the nails are overgrown, gradually pare them back. The quick will slowly recede, allowing you to trim them shorter, but this can take a couple of months.

The dewclaws don't come in contact with the ground and therefore need more frequent trimming. Situated high on the inside of the leg, they can be overlooked and will eventually grow all the way around and pierce the toe pad if not trimmed.

If you cut a nail too short, apply styptic powder, pressure, or ice for about 30 seconds until the bleeding stops. Do not soak or rinse the nail, which will slow clotting. And don't let your Poodle walk on it until you are sure that the bleeding has stopped.

Some owners prefer to use a nail grinder to trim their dogs' nails. If you want to try this, your Poodle's feet must be shaved first to prevent hair from getting caught in the spinning grinder wheel. Firmly support the paw in one hand and spread the toes slightly apart. Touch the grinder to the nail tip for a second or two, but do not apply pressure. Repeat to gradually shorten the nail.

How to Trim Your Poodle's Feet

If your Poodle is trained to have his nails trimmed, he will also allow you to remove the hair on his feet. Small, inexpensive clippers can be purchased from pet supply companies to perform this task. Put your dog in a sitting position facing you on the grooming table. Hold a paw firmly and work slowly, using a light touch. Hold the clipper level with the skin. For a close clip, you must shave against the grain of the hair. Shave the top of the foot from toes to ankle joint but no higher. To remove the hair on the bottom of the foot, separate the toes, push a finger up between the webbing, and run the clipper lightly over it in a side-to-side motion between the toes to the base of each nail.

Ear Care

Your dog's ears should be checked and cleaned weekly, which will help to prevent most of the ear problems that commonly afflict this breed. The canine ear canal is long, extending

SENIOR DOG TIP

Grooming the Older Dog

Grooming is important at every stage of your Poodle's life. Older dogs may no longer require a demanding grooming routine, but they still relish the attention, and it becomes even more important as a means of assessing daily condition. Your Poodle's routine may need modifications as he ages. Be patient and gentle, and keep grooming sessions short so that he does not become overly fatigued. A thinning coat and dry skin may signal a health problem such as hypothyroidism but also may be a normal aspect of aging. If your Poodle's skin becomes drier and more sensitive, less frequent bathing may help. He also may benefit from a moisturizing shampoo and conditioner or fatty acid supplements to restore natural oils to his skin.

Looking Good

downward from the opening to the level of the jaw before turning horizontally toward the eardrum. Foxtails, seeds, burs, moisture, bacteria, and debris can become trapped inside.

Because they are meant to hunt in dense underbrush and retrieve from water, Poodles have two features designed to protect their ears. Long ear leather and narrow ear canals help to prevent

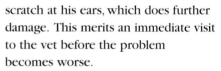

When removing hair from your Poodle's ears, be careful not to pinch his skin.

water and debris from getting in but can also restrict air circulation, creating an ideal environment for infections. The Poodle's legendary love for swimming also increases his risk of getting moisture in his ear canals, a problem comparable to "swimmer's ear." After swimming or bathing, dry his coat and the interior of his ears thoroughly, especially during hot damp weather.

Yeast and bacterial infections are the most common sources of canine ear trouble, characterized by reddish-brown debris and a strong odor. A small amount of yellowish ear wax in the canal is normal. Dark-colored, sweet-smelling debris and red, irritated ears indicate a problem. Minor ear infections can quickly turn serious because the intense discomfort causes the dog to

scratch at his ears, which does further damage. This merits an immediate visit to the vet before the problem becomes worse.

Normally, regular cleaning will head off most ear problems before they turn serious. Canine ear cleaning solution flushes out debris and creates a more acidic pH level inside the ear to discourage infection. Never use peroxide or rubbing alcohol to clean your Poodle's ears.

How to Clean Your Poodle's Ears

To clean your Poodle's ears, hold the ear leather open and squeeze enough solution in to fill the ear canal. Close the ear flap and massage it in for a few seconds. Do not let him shake his head, which can splash the solution into his eyes—or yours. It is not harmful, but it will sting. Use cotton balls to wipe any debris from the ear, but do not probe into the ear.

Sprinkle a small amount of ear powder into each ear after cleaning to make sure that the canals are completely dry.

How to Trim Your Poodle's Ear Hair

Poodles are prone to excess hair growth in their ear canals. This hair serves to keep debris out. Some Poodles are not bothered by it, and opinions vary about removing it. Excessive amounts can clog the ear canal, allowing moisture, dirt, and bacteria to build up. If it is causing a problem, you can remove it yourself. Fold back the ear flap, and sprinkle ear powder or baking soda onto the hair growing out of the ear canal to make it brittle and easier to grip. Grasp a few hairs firmly with your fingers, a pair of tweezers, or hemostat, and pull. It will come out easily and painlessly. Be careful not to pinch the skin of the ear or pull any hair growing on the ear flap or around the ear.

Eye Care

Check your Poodle's eyes daily for any irritation, tearing, or redness, which may require a vet visit. Keep in mind that he will be much less prone to eye irritation if you keep his topknot trimmed or tied up out of his face.

How to Clean Your Poodle's Eye Area

Use a dampened cotton ball to remove debris from the corners of his eyes and to wipe away any moisture buildup under his eyes that may cause staining.

Dental Care

You should brush your Poodle's teeth daily. Even if you don't manage it that

Hypoallergenic Breeds

Curly-coated breeds like the Poodle are often described as nonallergic, nonshedding, or hypoallergenic. These are subjective claims based on some facts about Poodle coats. It's true that the Poodle's coat has low hair density, produces limited amounts of dander, and undergoes minimal shedding. However, these traits are not guaranteed to prevent allergic reactions.

Proteins in canine saliva, urine, and shed skin cells (dander) all can help to aggravate an allergic response in a susceptible individual. Poodles are less likely than some other dogs to trigger an allergic response, but there is no way of knowing this for sure without long-term exposure to the breed. If you are allergic to dogs, do not acquire a Poodle without first spending enough time around the breed to confirm whether you are allergic to it.

often, do it before the plaque calcifies or works its way under the gum line. If it is not removed within a few days, it hardens into a dark brown substance known as tartar, which cannot be wiped off.

Removing heavy tartar buildup requires a visit to the vet. This is a fairly expensive procedure that includes the inevitable risks associated with anesthesia. However, it is essential to protect your Poodle's health. Periodontal disease can lead to painful dental abscesses, potentially fatal bacterial infections in major body

Wipe away any moisture buildup under your Poodle's eyes, or it can stain his coat.

organs, and erosion of the jawbone in Toy Poodles.

How to Brush Your Poodle's Teeth

Clean your dog's teeth with a gauze pad or doggy toothbrush and toothpaste or baking soda. Wipe the surface of each tooth using a circular motion, paying special attention to the gum line and spaces between the teeth. Hard foods, dental chews, tartar control biscuits, and dental sprays also can help to keep plaque formation under control.

Professional Grooming

Most owners opt to have their Poodles professionally groomed every six to eight weeks. Ask your pet-owning neighbors about grooming salons in your area, and don't be surprised if these opinions run the gamut from wonderful to abysmal. Professional groomers are not required to be licensed, but credentials from a nationally recognized organization are a definite plus. This certification may be issued by the International Professional Groomers, Inc. (IPG), the International Society of Canine Cosmetologists (ISCC), the National Dog Groomers Association of America (NDGAA), or the World Wide Pet Supply Association (WWPSA). Certified groomers are also more likely to keep their skills up to par by attending conferences, seminars, and competitions.

Don't hesitate to drop in to look around a few grooming shops before deciding to leave your Poodle for the day. That is your best assurance that the environment is clean and safe. You may need to call in advance, but groomers should permit you to see where the dogs are kept and exercised. The premises should have security precautions to prevent accidental injuries or escapes, and the staff should have procedures in place to handle possible emergencies.

Professional grooming fees are usually based on the size of the dog. Ask for price quotes for full grooming, including a bath, fluff dry, and trimming, and ask whether they charge extra for nail clipping and ear cleaning.

Regular visits to a grooming salon will minimize the work you have to do at home, but it won't exempt you from the routine entirely. In between visits, your Poodle will need regular maintenance, including brushing, ear and teeth cleaning, nail clipping, and occasionally bathing. The good news is that centuries of selective breeding have made the Poodle one of the most biddable breeds to groom. The vast

Grooming the Curly Coat

Curly coats require more than average grooming. The hair constantly grows and must be trimmed at regular intervals to maintain a tidy appearance. Frequent bathing and brushing are essential to remove dead hair and prevent mats. The amount of actual work involved in grooming your Poodle will be determined by his coat. An ideal coat should be uniformly thick, harsh, and curly for maximum protection and minimum grooming. Poodles have very little undercoat, and the outercoat should comprise coarse-textured curly hair.

majority of them enjoy it. Even less enthusiastic customers willingly tolerate it. Professional groomers are usually delighted to work with Poodles because of their cooperative attitude.

Grooming is an essential aspect of Poodle ownership, and the proper attitude makes a world of difference. The majority of Poodle owners quickly discover that it's an enjoyable pastime rather than a chore.

Chapter 5

Feeling Good

A preventive health program is an integral part of your Poodle's general care and includes much more than making sure that his shots are up to date. This chapter covers health care basics, including how to select a good vet, neutering, vaccinations, parasites, common disorders and diseases, emergencies, and alternative therapies.

Selecting a Qualified Vet

Owners are regularly advised to find a vet before acquiring a new Poodle. This is wise, but you won't realize its full importance until your dog faces a health crisis. In a situation like that, the possibility of indifferent, incompetent, or impersonal care will matter tremendously.

Ask for Recommendations

An easy way to start your search is simply to ask your dog-owning neighbors for recommendations. When you have a few names, call and inquire about fees, payment options, which health insurance plans are accepted, and what kind of emergency care they offer.

Visit the Clinic

Of course, even if the phone interview goes well, you may change your mind after seeing the place.

Veterinary clinics vary greatly in ambiance and service. Your Poodle may get equally good care in a small general practice office and in a large clinic, but you need to feel comfortable there as well. A few key factors can ensure this:

- The premises must be clean, calm, and welcoming. Coping with an ill pet is tremendously stressful, and the atmosphere of your veterinary clinic should ease this feeling rather than exacerbate it.
- Same day appointments and after-hours emergency care are essential services. Dogs do not schedule their illnesses in advance.
- Don't underestimate the importance of competent, friendly vet techs and office staff. Regardless of the vet's demeanor or skill, she will have a tremendous impact on your overall experience.

Take an Active Role in Your Dog's Care

Taking an active role in your Poodle's health care includes participating in decision-making. Impersonal service or a personality clash can make this difficult. You should never feel hesitant discussing treatment options or the potential risks and costs of medications or procedures. However, this becomes more difficult if you see a different vet every visit. That won't happen at a

Even a healthy dog will require an annual checkup at his vet.

small private practice, but you may face delays while important tests are sent out to labs or be referred to specialists for unusual problems. Whichever you choose, it is far easier to mull over these options when little Bruno is not in the midst of a health emergency.

The Annual Health Exam

Even if your Poodle is in picture-perfect health, he needs an annual checkup. This normally includes checking temperature, respiratory and heart rates, and body weight. His mouth will be checked for periodontal disease, and his skin, coat, and ears will be examined for parasites and bacterial infections. Depending on his age and current health, your vet may suggest blood testing, fecal testing, urinalysis, or X-rays as part of the checkup. She also may make recommendations about diet and nutrition based on your Poodle's weight and condition.

The annual exam should not automatically include vaccinations or a teeth cleaning under full anesthesia. These treatments are not always necessary—or risk free. Extra vaccinations won't enhance your Poodle's immunity and may actually undermine it. Also, a dog's liver needs several weeks to metabolize the toxins in a dose of anesthesia. If his liver function is compromised for any reason, the toxins can build up, causing anesthesia toxicity.

55

Feeling Good

After age seven, biannual health checks for your Poodle are advisable. Age-related problems like heart or kidney disease don't always cause obvious symptoms until they are advanced. Your vet also will be able to spot suspicious lumps or growths that might signal early stages of cancer. Early detection is your Poodle's best guarantee of successful treatment and continued good health.

Neutering

Most puppies are neutered around five or six months of age. This is based on convention rather than research showing that this is the best age for the procedure. Both large and small Poodles may benefit by waiting until they are slightly older. This reduces the risks associated with anesthesia and surgery for Toys and ensures complete bone growth in Standards.

Neutering is a routine procedure, but it does require full anesthesia, which is never risk free. Gas anesthetic, such as isoflorane, is safest. Before surgery, you will be asked to withhold food and water from your Poodle for eight hours.

Most dogs are up on their feet a few hours after surgery, but the vet may want to keep your Poodle for observation overnight. After bringing him home, his activities should be restricted for several days. Analgesics can minimize post-surgical pain and speed recovery. Complications are rare, most commonly minor infections or swelling caused by licking the incision. In that case, your Poodle may be fitted with an Elizabethan collar until healing is complete.

Vaccinations

A vaccine contains minute amounts of a specific bacteria or virus. These are introduced into the body to stimulate antibody resistance to that disease. If a vaccinated individual is exposed to that particular disease in the future, his immune system will "remember" and trigger an immediate response to fight it off.

Vaccines are generally classified as "core" and "noncore." Core vaccines are considered essential, while noncore vaccines are optional. Core vaccines protect against distemper, parvovirus, adenovirus 2 (hepatitis), and rabies. Noncore vaccines include bordetella (kennel cough), coronavirus, borrelia burgdorferi (Lyme disease), leptospirosis, and giardia. The value of a noncore vaccine depends on your Poodle's environment and lifestyle.

If you acquire your Poodle as a puppy, he will need a series of three vaccinations beginning when he is eight weeks old. This is known as the DHPP shot, which immunizes a dog against distemper, hepatitis, parainfluenza, and parvovirus.

After a puppy is vaccinated, his disease resistance develops gradually. Some puppies may not be protected until receiving their third shot. This is why it's important to keep little Bruno away from other dogs during these weeks. Dog parks, boarding kennels, pet shops, vets offices, and the like can present a risk to unvaccinated puppies.

Diseases to Vaccinate Against

Vaccinations are not usually administered individually. This would entail a minimum of 12 shots for each puppy and most owners (and puppies) prefer to minimize this. Most commonly, distemper, hepatitis, leptospirosis, parvovirus, and parainfluenza vaccines are given in one combined injection, referred to as a "puppy shot." However, a wide range of commercially produced vaccines allow this practice to be customized to a dog's particular needs.

The following are some descriptions of diseases against which dog are commonly vaccinated.

Distemper
Thanks to vaccinations, distemper is rare today. But it is highly contagious and still poses a risk for unvaccinated puppies. The virus is transmitted through contact with droplets from infected dogs. Early symptoms usually include fever, depression, anorexia, diarrhea, and nasal and ocular discharge. Bronchitis and pneumonia are common complications. Other than supportive care, there is no effective treatment.

Hepatitis
Infectious canine hepatitis (ICH) is a highly contagious viral disease that may strike dogs of any age, but puppies are at

highest risk. It is transmitted by contact with urine, feces, or the saliva of infected dogs. ICH can manifest as sudden severe bloody diarrhea, depression, vomiting, conjunctivitis, tonsillitis, anorexia, or jaundice. Treatment consists of supportive care.

Kennel Cough
Kennel cough is caused by various strains of airborne parainfluenza viruses and bordetella bacteria. The resulting upper respiratory infection causes a harsh, hacking cough. Infections are usually self-limiting, running their course in a week, but kennel cough can develop into pneumonia in puppies. Pet shops, kennels, and shelters are common sources of infection. Inhalant (intranasal) vaccines are considered

Starting at eight weeks of age, all puppies receive a series of vaccinations against distemper, hepatitis, parainfluenza, and parvovirus.

most effective. The parainfluenza component of the DHPP vaccination also provides protection.

Parainfluenza

Parainfluenza encompasses several viral strains that cause kennel cough. (See "Kennel Cough" for more information.)

Parvovirus

Parvovirus first made headlines in the 1970s, and outbreaks of this highly contagious virus continue to threaten canine populations everywhere. It is transmitted by contact with minute traces of infectious fecal matter. Symptoms include sudden severe depression, vomiting, bloody diarrhea, and extreme dehydration. Dogs of any age are susceptible. It is usually fatal to puppies; prognosis is guarded for adults. Treatment includes supportive therapy to combat dehydration and shock.

Rabies

Thanks to vaccination, rabies is now almost unknown in humans or canines in the US. But it still infects wildlife in many parts of the country. Without immediate treatment, this disease is invariably fatal. It is transmitted through contact with the saliva of an infected animal—the animal doesn't necessarily have to bite or scratch its victim. Altered behavior is one of the earliest symptoms, and wild animals acting unusually fearless, friendly, or lethargic should raise suspicion. Irritability, depression, fever, vomiting, and diarrhea are typical symptoms.

When to Vaccinate

The series of three DHPP vaccinations should be administered at least three weeks apart to ensure optimum immune response. Many

Extreme lethargy or depression may be signs of illness, so take your Poodle to the vet if he exhibits these signs.

breeders recommend giving an antihistamine shot immediately before each one to minimize potential reactions.

Many veterinary organizations began backing off the idea of annual revaccinations in 2001 and now advocate booster shots every three years. Some owners prefer to rely on antibody titer levels to determine if or when booster shots are needed. This blood test can be done annually as part of your Poodle's checkup.

The rabies vaccination is the only immunization that dogs are legally required to have. It should never be given in combination with DHPP because it can overload a puppy's immune system, increasing the risk for vaccine failure or adverse reactions. Most breeders recommend waiting until a puppy is at least six months old before administering a rabies vaccination. A puppy's immune system is mature by six months of age, vastly increasing the likelihood of a maximum immune response to the vaccine.

Vaccination Risks

Illness and stress can interfere with the body's ability to effectively respond to a vaccination. For this reason, shots should not be given immediately before or after a stressful experience, before or after surgery, or during recovery from an illness.

The possible risks of vaccines are far outweighed by the protection they provide against potentially fatal illnesses. Some of these illnesses are treatable, some are not. Even recovered dogs often suffer permanent side effects such as neurological impairment or organ damage.

The Expert Knows

Dental Chew Toys

Even though dogs love them and they help to remove plaque from teeth, both vets and manufacturers recommend giving dental chews only under supervision. The major risk is respiratory or gastrointestinal blockage from swallowing large chewed pieces. Hard plastic chews are considered safer, but it is still possible for a dog to chew off and swallow pieces. The plastic bits are indigestible, and a resulting blockage may be hard to spot on X-rays. Despite manufacturer claims, there is no such thing as an indestructible chew toy. When selecting chews for your Poodle, larger is always safer than smaller, especially if you have multiple dogs working on them. Always discard them when they begin to show signs of wear or dirt.

Parasites

Unless you keep your dog in a hermetically sealed environment, he will be exposed to a range of internal and external parasites throughout his life. However, most parasites don't cause serious problems if detected and treated early.

Internal Parasites

The most common internal parasites are heartworms, hookworms, roundworms, tapeworms, and whipworms. Your Poodle can easily pick up these or other less common internal parasites, although the effects may not become noticeable until the infestation is severe.

There are plenty of effective medications available to treat them, but don't administer these medications unless you are certain they are necessary. Treatment for any parasite is potentially toxic. Fecal testing by your vet should be part of your Poodle's annual health check. If a problem is detected, he will prescribe the safest, most effective medication for that particular parasite. That, however, won't solve the problem unless you stop the source of infestation, which may range from contaminated soil, fleas, or infected wildlife in the area.

Heartworms

Heartworms are transmitted by mosquitoes. Infected dogs don't suffer obvious effects until the worm larvae migrate to the heart and grow large enough to impede cardiac function. Early stages

of infection are diagnosed through blood testing. Heartworm is found in every state in the US. Depending on where you live, your Poodle should receive a seasonal or year-round preventive. His blood must be tested before starting a seasonal preventive.

Hookworms

Hookworms are more widespread in warm, damp climates but are certainly not limited to these regions. Hookworms cause weight loss, anemia, and bloody or blackish diarrhea.

Roundworms

Many puppies are born with roundworms, and they are transmissible to humans. Symptoms include intermittent vomiting and diarrhea, weight loss, pot-bellied appearance, and spaghetti-like worms in vomit or feces.

Depending on where you live, your Poodle should receive a seasonal or year-round heartworm preventive.

Tapeworms

Tapeworms are prevalent wherever fleas are a problem. Symptoms include failure to gain weight despite a healthy appetite, intermittent diarrhea, and the presence of tiny tapeworm segments shed intermittently in feces.

Whipworms

Like hookworms, whipworms are more common in warm, damp climates. Whipworms inhabit the large intestine, causing diarrhea, weight loss, and anemia.

Check your dog for external parasites, like fleas and ticks, after he's been playing outside.

External Parasites

External parasites include fleas and ticks.

Fleas

The main rule of flea control is that prevention is far easier than eradication. Fleas are hard to spot, especially on dark-colored Poodles. One or two can turn your house into a flea festival before you notice anything. Get in the habit of checking your Poodle for these creatures, especially if he begins scratching or chewing at his coat. A tip-off is the presence of gritty black flea dirt (flea feces) on his skin.

Some dogs are highly allergic to the proteins in flea saliva. In fact, flea bites are one of the most common causes of hot spots, sores caused by severe itching and inflammation. Topical or oral cortisone can temporarily relieve the symptoms and break the cycle, but this condition, sometimes called flea bite dermatitis, is likely to recur unless the flea problem is controlled.

Getting rid of the fleas on your Poodle won't do much good if you don't treat his environment at the same time. One flea represents 10 percent of an active infestation. Effective flea control must include eradicating fleas and eggs from bedding, furniture, rugs, shrubbery, and grass. Flea control products include dips, sprays, powders, baths, and oral and topical preventives. These should be used only under your vet's supervision and never in combination. For Toy Poodles, topical preventives for cats are preferred.

Before initiating a war on fleas, consider potential safety factors. For example, combining multiple products can cause a toxic reaction. Also, many breeders caution against using flea products containing the insecticide carbaryl on Poodles.

Ticks

If ticks are a problem in your area, check for them every time you groom your Poodle. When you find one, pull it off with tweezers or a hemostat. Never use kerosene, gasoline, or a lit match to remove a tick.

Most ticks are harmless, but tick-borne diseases are becoming more prevalent. Canine Lyme disease, spread by the deer tick, is the most common. Dogs in high-risk areas can be vaccinated against Lyme disease, but it is not guaranteed to provide complete protection. Less common tick-borne illnesses include Rocky Mountain spotted fever and ehrlichiosis. If you suspect that your Poodle may have contracted one of these illnesses, get a blood test. Prompt antibiotic therapy can make a big difference in the outcome.

Common Poodle Disorders and Diseases

Hundreds of genetically based disorders have been documented in dogs, and every breed is prone to one or more of them. That doesn't imply that all Poodles are at risk, though. In fact, a well-bred Poodle is unlikely to develop any of them. Modern research has provided an ever-increasing arsenal of tools to identify and eradicate health disorders, and careful breeders utilize them all.

Addison's Disease

Addison's disease (hypoadreno-corticism) is caused by insufficient adrenal hormones. The adrenal glands produce several hormones that are key to many aspects of body function. These hormones regulate stress tolerance, immune function, and metabolism; they also help the body efficiently utilize fats, proteins, and carbohydrates. Addison's disease can affect all three sizes of Poodles but is seen most frequently in Standards.

Regular veterinary care can keep your Poodle healthy for years to come.

SENIOR DOG TIP

Your Senior Poodle's Health

You can expect to enjoy your Poodle's company for 12 to 15 years, but keep in mind that physical and mental changes come with the old age package. Gradual loss of muscle mass and bone density may not be obvious but will lessen his interest in active pursuits. Arthritis can make him reluctant to go for walks, climb stairs, or jump off furniture. If he seems restless at night or stiff when he gets up in the morning, an orthopedic cushion or heating pad might help. Pain medications may be advisable, but consult your vet before giving any nonprescription products.

Older Poodles also may suffer from diminished sight or hearing. Both may go undetected until they become fairly advanced. Dogs are adept at compensating for vision loss, especially if in a familiar environment. Early signs of hearing loss are also subtle. He may fail to come when called or become difficult to rouse from a deep sleep.

Vision or hearing loss or physical pain also can lead to behavioral changes like confusion, crankiness, or housetraining lapses. Cognitive dysfunction syndrome is another possible reason for sudden behavior changes in an elderly Poodle. This disorder may be the underlying cause of chronic restlessness, hyperactivity, sudden anxiety, fearfulness, or aggression. Experimental trials with drugs used to treat Parkinson's disease in humans have shown promising results in controlling some cases of cognitive dysfunction syndrome in dogs.

Symptoms

Early symptoms of Addison's disease include lethargy, vomiting, poor coat condition, and lack of appetite.

Stress can trigger severe symptoms because the adrenal glands cannot respond with normal cortisol production. This can result in impaired heart function, arrhythmia, and occasionally sudden heart failure due to abnormally high potassium levels.

Treatment

Blood tests showing ratios of low sodium and high potassium levels can confirm some cases of Addison's, but the ACTH response test, which confirms whether the body is producing adrenal hormone, is the most accurate diagnostic test.

Treatment consists of medical management with oral fludrocortisones acetate and prednisone to replace natural adrenal hormones.

Bloat

Bloat, also known as gastric dilatation volvulus (GVD) and gastric torsion, is more common in large breeds like the Standard Poodle. This is an emergency condition in which the stomach becomes painfully distended and rotates, trapping the contents and cutting off blood supply.

Symptoms

Symptoms include anxiety, restlessness, whining and panting, gagging, salivating, shallow breathing, rapid heart rate,

weak pulse, abnormal color of the mucous membranes, and noticeable distension of the abdomen.

Treatment

Without immediate treatment, bloat can lead to potentially fatal shock within 6 to 12 hours. Treatment includes immediate gastric decompression, IV fluids to combat shock, and broad-spectrum antibiotics to prevent endotoxemia.

Bloat cannot be prevented, but susceptible dogs should be fed small meals of a high-quality low fiber food at least three times daily, and physical activity and excitement should be avoided before, during, and for several hours after eating.

Cushing's Disease

Cushing's disease is caused by the overproduction of cortisone. It has been documented in all three sizes of Poodles. Produced by the adrenal glands, cortisone normally regulates blood glucose levels, fat production, protein metabolism, and enhances immune function. This disease is rarely seen in dogs under five years of age.

Cushing's can be caused by cancer, a pituitary gland tumor, an adrenal gland tumor, or the overuse of oral or topical steroid drugs. Diabetes is a common secondary complication of this disease.

Symptoms

Typical symptoms of Cushing's are excessive thirst, increased urination, constant hunger, bloated abdomen, pattern baldness along the flanks, muscle wasting, flaking and/or thickening of the skin, and lethargy.

Treatment

Diagnosis is confirmed through blood tests. Medication is usually recommended.

Epilepsy

Seizures can be inherited or caused by trauma, metabolic disorders, infectious diseases, or toxins. If a seizure occurs and no cause can be determined, it is known as idiopathic epilepsy. Epilepsy has been documented in Toy, Miniature, and Standard Poodles.

Symptoms

A seizure may occur without warning, or it may be preceded by twitching, tremors, and staring, or noticeably restless, panicky behaviors such as circling, panting, whining, and pacing. This quickly progresses to chewing movements, salivation, drooling, incontinence, muscle spasms, stiffening of the extremities, and convulsions.

Treatment

If your Poodle experiences a seizure only occasionally, treatment may not be necessary. If they occur regularly or last longer than five minutes, they should be treated. Most cases can be controlled with phenobarbitol, potassium bromide, or a combination of both drugs. Long-term or lifetime medication is often necessary.

Some conditions, such as epilepsy, can be found in Standard, Miniature (not pictured), and Toy Poodles.

Hip Dysplasia

Hip dysplasia is a genetic malformation of the hip's ball and socket joints. Deformity can range from mild, causing no symptoms, to crippling. This condition can affect Toys, Minis, and Standards.

Symptoms

Early symptoms include reluctance to exercise, stiffness, especially after sleeping, a swaying or hopping gait, and muscle wasting in the hind legs.

Treatment

Diagnosis is confirmed through an X-ray. Mild cases may respond to anti-inflammatory pain medication, controlled exercise, and dietary management to prevent excess weight gain from causing unnecessary stress on joints. In severe cases, surgical replacement of the joint may be necessary.

Hypothyroidism

Hypothyroidism results from an insufficient production of thyroid hormone, which is crucial to regulating numerous body functions, including growth and maturation. Hypothyroidism has been documented in all sizes of Poodles.

Symptoms

Symptoms usually appear in dogs who are between

Vomiting and Diarrhea

Every dog experiences bouts of vomiting and diarrhea sometime in his life. Common reasons include overeating, eating or drinking too fast, sudden dietary changes, travel sickness, or eating indigestible substances. If your Poodle repeatedly drinks and vomits, he may experience additional fluid loss and possibly shock. Temporarily withhold water until his stomach settles. After two hours, offer small amounts of water frequently to prevent dehydration, but don't let him gulp too much at once. You also can offer him ice cubes to lick or a pediatric glucose drink to correct potential electrolyte imbalance.

Wait 12 hours before starting your dog on a bland diet of lean boiled chicken or hamburger and rice. Give small portions until you are certain that his stomach can handle it, and don't force him to eat if he is not ready. Gradually resume feeding his normal diet over a period of three days. It's time for a trip to the vet if:

- symptoms persist for more than a day
- your dog also experiences weakness, pain, or fever
- the diarrhea or vomit contains blood

four to ten years old and include weight gain, lethargy, dry skin, patterned hair thinning, and baldness.

Treatment

This is the most commonly diagnosed endocrine disorder in dogs. Diagnosis is confirmed through a blood test, although the accuracy of current tests remains controversial. A second opinion may be warranted before starting your Poodle on synthetic thyroid hormone.

Legg-Calve-Perthes Disease

Legg-Calve-Perthes disease is hereditary and can affect Toy and Miniature Poodles. A compromised blood supply to the ball of the hip joint causes bone degeneration, muscle wasting, pain, and limping.

Symptoms

Symptoms are similar to those caused by hip dysplasia—reluctance to exercise, stiffness, a swaying or hopping gait, and muscle wasting in the hind legs—and become apparent around three months of age. One or both hind legs may be affected.

Treatment

Diagnosis is confirmed by an X-ray. In less serious cases, confinement and anti-inflammatory drugs should be tried for at least one month before

Patellar luxation is common in both Toy and Mini Poodles; surgery may be recommended to correct the problem.

resorting to surgery. Most dogs recover complete use of the leg following surgery but will need physical therapy for several weeks to ensure this. If both legs require surgery, the second should not be done until complete function has returned to the first leg. Otherwise, the dog risks permanently losing function of both legs.

Patellar Luxation

Patellar luxation, a condition in which the kneecap luxates (dislocates) and slides to the inside or outside of the leg, can affect Toy and Miniature Poodles. This is a common orthopedic problem in dogs who weigh less than 20 pounds (9.1 kg). It is not a painful condition, but the effects can range from mild to crippling. Arthritis is a common secondary complication.

Feeling Good

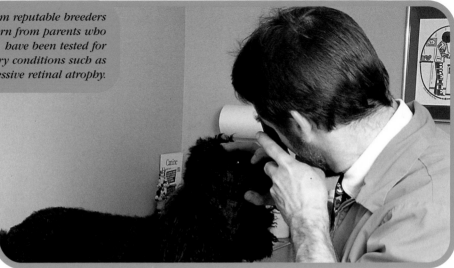

Symptoms

When luxation occurs, the dog cannot fully extend the leg and will hop or skip until it pops back into place. In severe cases, he will not be able to bear weight on the affected joint, which will cause him to shift his weight frequently or stand bowlegged.

Most affected Poodles are predisposed to the problem by one or more deformities of the knee joint, which are occasionally caused by injury. The defect is present at birth but may not cause symptoms for months or years. One quarter of cases show symptoms in both knees, although one is usually more seriously affected than the other.

Treatment

Surgical correction is sometimes recommended, but successful repair is contingent on the dog's general health, the severity of deformity, and the extent of joint degeneration.

Progressive Retinal Atrophy (PRA)

PRA includes seven hereditary eye diseases found in all three sizes of Poodles. Progressive rod-cone degeneration (PRCD) is the most common form affecting Toys and Minis, but so far, it has not been confirmed in Standards. (But Standard Poodles are susceptible to other types of PRA.) All forms of PRA cause gradual deterioration of the cells of the retina, leading to blindness. The age of onset varies. PRCD can cause noticeable vision deterioration by age 3, while other forms may start causing vision loss between 5 and 12 years of age, although they usually can be diagnosed at an earlier age.

Symptoms

PRA is not painful, and it is not accompanied by any visible changes in the eye such as redness or clouding. The earliest sign is often a change in the dog's behavior. He may become reluctant to go out at night due to night blindness, or he may become inexplicably apprehensive in a strange place. An eye exam is always recommended in the case of sudden behavioral changes in a young healthy dog. At later stages of retinal degeneration, the pupils may appear dilated. In some cases, cataracts start to form in later stages of PRA.

Treatment

Diagnosis must be done by a canine ophthalmologist. There is no treatment for PRA, only supportive care.

Legitimate Poodle breeders routinely screen their dogs for PRA. When purchasing a Poodle puppy, make sure that the parents are certified free of eye disorders.

Sebaceous Adenitis (SA)

Sebaceous adenitis (SA) is an inherited skin disease that destroys the sebaceous glands, causing coat loss, thickened skin, and secondary skin infections. All three Poodle sizes can be affected, but it is most prevalent in Standards. Up to 50 percent of all Standard Poodles are estimated to be carriers or affected by SA. This condition can affect dogs as young as one and a half or as old as nine years.

Symptoms

Early symptoms include silvery dandruff, musty skin odor, and a thinning coat.

Treatment

This disease is sometimes misdiagnosed as hypothyroidism or allergies, so a skin biopsy is needed for definite diagnosis. There is no effective cure for SA. Treatment to

Disaster Preparedness

Devise a disaster plan for pets in case of fire, flood, or emergency evacuation. Here are some basics:

1. Prepare kits of supplies, and store them in an accessible location. Include basic dog essentials like food, water, bedding, leash, first-aid kit and medications, and micro-chip and vaccination records.
2. Have a carrier for each pet labeled with your contact information, including cell phone numbers.
3. Map out alternative escape routes and safe havens where dogs will be welcomed.

During an emergency, pets may become nervous, disoriented, or unpredictable. Keep them leashed or crated, and make sure that they wear collars and tags.

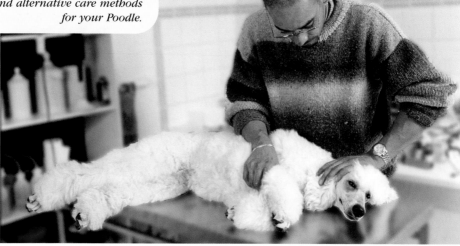

You may want to consider a combination of conventional and alternative care methods for your Poodle.

Poodles

control symptoms includes oil baths to moisturize the skin and remove excess dandruff and antibiotics to control secondary infections.

von Willebrand's Disease (vWD)

Von Willebrand's disease (vWD) includes several related bleeding disorders caused by lowered levels of von Willebrand's factor. This resultant abnormal platelet function causes excessive prolonged bleeding.

Symptoms

Symptoms can range from mild to severe. Mildly affected dogs experience occasional episodes of prolonged bleeding in response to events like teething, surgery, or traumatic injuries. Stress and drugs such as aspirin will worsen symptoms.

Treatment

Poodles are at risk for Type 1 vWD, which can be diagnosed through a blood test. There is no cure for this disease.

Health Emergencies

Health emergencies can range from a broken toenail to a broken leg, or worse. Whether the emergency is major or minor, your immediate response will have a big impact on the outcome. Get a book on canine first aid, or take a course to familiarize yourself with the basics. Knowing how to stop bleeding, recognize shock, and administer CPR or the Heimlich maneuver can save your Poodle's life. You also must know how to safely stabilize an injured dog before transporting him to the vet.

You can buy a canine first-aid kit, but assembling your own customized version may be more useful.

Suggested items include:
- antibiotic ointment
- Benadryl
- blunt-tipped scissors
- eye wash
- first-aid manual
- gauze, bandages, first-aid tape, a roll of sterile cotton
- hydrogen peroxide and rubbing alcohol
- Karo syrup or pediatric glucose solution
- over-the-counter remedies for vomiting and diarrhea
- telephone number of the poison control hotline (888-426-4435)
- telephone numbers of your regular vet and the emergency vet
- thermometer
- tweezers

Alternative Therapies

Many vets offer both conventional and alternative care options and don't hesitate to recommend them for conditions like chronic pain, seizure disorders, or spinal cord injuries, where conventional treatment possibilities are limited. Acupuncture, homeopathy, massage therapy, herbal medicine, and nutritional therapy can be a lifeline in such cases. Keep in mind that practitioners in these areas may or may not be licensed. They should, however, have a background in animal rather than human health care. Research is crucial before jumping on the alternative therapy bandwagon.

It is your responsibility to decide whether an alternative treatment is the right choice for your Poodle. Likewise, if your Poodle is undergoing alternative treatment, you must monitor his progress. A dog's response to alternative therapies is generally slower and less obvious than the typical response to conventional treatment. That doesn't necessarily mean that it's not working, but patience should never give way to wishful thinking.

For additional information on alternative therapies, visit:
- www.avcadoctors.com (American Veterinary Chiropractic Association)
- www.ahvma.org (American Holistic Veterinary Medical Association)
- www.ivas.org (International Veterinary Acupuncture Society)
- www.ahvma.org (American Holistic Veterinary Medical Association)

This chapter outlines the basics of your Poodle's health maintenance. It may seem like a lot of responsibility, but the returns on this investment are priceless.

Chapter 6

Being Good

For centuries, Poodles have reigned as the superstars of training. Quick learners and eager to please, they have tremendous training potential. However, it's up to you to provide your dog with opportunities to utilize it.

Don't assume that training isn't necessary because he is destined to be only your pet. Every dog needs guidance and boundaries to enjoy a happy life among the human race.

It's hard to imagine that your angelic Poodle is capable of getting into much trouble. But the fact is that your Poodle did not come equipped with a halo and wings—and it's more than likely that he will join the ranks of canine delinquents unless you train him. He can learn a lot on his own but depends on you, his pack leader, to understand how to communicate effectively and behave in socially acceptable ways toward people and other dogs.

The Importance of Positive Training

Positive training, which uses motivators like praise and treats to achieve results, is the best way to train your Poodle. Praise is a great way to get your Poodle's attention but won't always keep him focused during training—treats are the most effective tool for this. However, positive training involves more than constantly enticing your dog with food. As your Poodle gets the message, give them less predictably or vary them with less potent incentives like petting. Rewards are meant to maintain motivation, but overdoing it can simply make your dog bored with the whole routine.

Don't Use Negative Reinforcement

Negative reinforcement such as scolding will certainly put an immediate stop to your Poodle's unwanted behavior, but it almost never leads to any lasting improvement. One of the dog's basic survival skills is the ability to quickly form mental associations between actions and rewards. Negative reinforcement will encourage him to change a behavior, but positive reinforcement will encourage him to remember and repeat a specific behavior.

The Expert Knows

Treats and Training

Irresistible treats are a trainer's best friend because dogs are instinctively programmed to make connections between specific actions and rewards. When teaching a complicated concept, such as housetraining, treats can dramatically reinforce desired behavior that might otherwise take quite a while. Make sure that the treats are delectable and healthy, such as bite-sized cheese cubes, chicken bits, chopped turkey franks, and unsweetened cereal. Rotate them to keep your pet interested.

When socializing your dog, make sure that all interactions with other dogs are positive; remove him from the situation if he appears frightened or intimidated.

Be an Effective Leader

Some owners mistakenly assume that discipline undermines the bonding process. In fact, teaching your Poodle rules and boundaries reassures him of his place in your pack. His resulting sense of security bolsters his confidence and strengthens his trust in you.

When your Poodle misbehaves, sternly tell him "No." It should never be excessively harsh, emotional, or accompanied by physical punishment. Done once using an effective tone and stance will get your point across.

Never allow your dog to ignore you. On the other hand, if you haphazardly and halfheartedly enforce rules, he will soon learn to disregard them. His misbehavior will escalate, as will your negative reaction. Discipline will disintegrate into nonstop nagging, and he will become adept at tuning it out.

Socialization

Before you can teach your Poodle anything, you must be able to communicate effectively with each other. Establishing communication is the first step in training, and it is accomplished through regular social interaction. Socialization teaches your Poodle how to interact with the rest of the world.

It's up to you to supervise these social interactions to ensure that they are positive. Never allow your Poodle to become frightened or intimidated by older, larger dogs. Puppies are often guilty of inappropriate social behavior simply because they don't yet know

Being Good

any better. But don't let your puppy's occasional social faux pas make him a target for other dogs.

Constant supervision is especially important when introducing your Poodle to children and other pets. First introductions can set the stage for a lifetime relationship, good or bad.

How to Socialize Your Puppy

Puppies begin learning basic social skills within weeks of birth, but they need extensive experiences to perfect these skills. Have your puppy interact with a wide variety of people and other dogs from the time he is eight weeks old. He has a natural desire to explore and learn during these weeks, and his curiosity and learning potential are at their highest during this time.

This window doesn't remain open forever, so you must make the most of it. Use caution to ensure his safety before he is completely vaccinated, but don't wait to begin socializing him until his shots are completed at 16 weeks. Until your puppy is completely vaccinated, avoid places frequented by dogs such as dog runs or dog shows, and always keep him in your lap at the vet's waiting room. He can safely be exposed to human environments during these weeks. Take him for car rides, or explore public places such as your local mall or town square. Take him to visit a friend, and invite friends and relatives to your home to meet him.

FAMILY-FRIENDLY TIP

Children and Training

Involving your child in the training process has multiple benefits. Both child and dog learn mutual respect, concentration, and discipline. Your child also will learn how to properly communicate with your Poodle to get results. A junior dog training class is a great way to introduce a child to the basics, but most children find it equally rewarding to help with this at home. Your child can start by helping to praise the dog for a job well done during training sessions.

How to Socialize Your Adolescent

Your Poodle may become less willing to spontaneously socialize as he approaches adolescence and may need extra encouragement after four months of age. This is a great time to enroll him in puppy kindergarten or a basic training class; either will provide both of you with professional training guidance but also will give your Poodle regular social encounters with humans and canines.

How to Socialize Your Poodle to Children

Children generally have no inhibitions about making friends with a strange dog, so it's important to teach your child how to properly approach a dog and interpret his reaction for the child's own safety. Unless your Poodle has been raised with children, he will need time to become accustomed to a child's mannerisms and demeanor. A dog can misinterpret a young child's normal exuberance.

The initial introduction should be closely supervised by an adult. If the child is getting acquainted with a young puppy, it's safer to have them sit on the floor. Show the child how to reassuringly encourage the puppy with praise, petting, and treats. At this stage,

don't let either party get overexcited or rambunctious. A large Poodle could accidentally injure a small child roughhousing. Likewise, a child could hurt a Toy Poodle. Children should understand that it is never okay to chase or tease a dog. Poodles are incredibly patient and sweet tempered, but any dog will bite if sufficiently frightened or provoked. Your child should respect the dog's need to retreat to his bed or crate and understand that he is off-limits at those times.

How to Socialize Your Poodle to Household Pets

Poodles have a well-deserved reputation for easygoing sociability. Even so, introducing a Poodle into a

Proper socialization will teach your Poodle to get along well both with humans and other animals.

multi-pet household requires advance planning. Some pets hit it off immediately, and others need days or weeks to accept each other. Either way, supervise all interactions and keep them separated whenever this isn't possible. A Toy Poodle can be accidentally injured by a playful large dog.

Dogs

When introducing your Poodle to another dog, observe their body language carefully. The encounter may start off fine with tail wagging and sniffing, but be prepared to stop the visit if either dog shows signs of fearfulness or aggression. Given time, most dogs develop a good relationship. Don't force them to socialize before they are ready, though. And don't incite jealousy by encouraging them to share beds, toys, or food. Respect each dog's space, and never give the impression of favoring the newcomer.

Cats

Cats and dogs can be the best of friends or lifelong enemies. In part, this depends on their early social experiences with other species. By nature, dogs are more extroverted. Cats vary in their desire to socialize. If your cat plainly wants nothing to do with your Poodle, it is best to give them their own space and accept the situation. If they seem interested in a

Canine Communication

Regardless of how smart your Poodle may be, he won't learn a thing unless he is paying attention. To keep his attention focused on you, conduct training sessions in a calm, relaxed manner. Use clear, deliberate gestures and an encouraging vocal tone to communicate a sense of assurance. If your Poodle seems nervous, overexcited, or distracted, try combining verbal commands and hand gestures to hold his attention. The ability to focus on training takes practice, especially for a puppy. Treats can be a great attention getter, but some dogs find this too distracting and may work better for praise. Regular interaction is the secret to discovering which techniques work best for your Poodle.

mutual friendship, encourage this with supervised visits. The cat should always have some escape route in case she becomes annoyed or frightened by the dog. A cornered, defensive cat can seriously hurt a small dog.

Crate Training

Crate training—training your dog to accept going into his crate on command—should never be perceived as banishment to a cage. That is human misinterpretation of both dog behavior and training. Dogs instinctively seek a safe den, and crate training builds on this canine instinct. If you acquired your puppy from a breeder, he was probably familiarized with the security of a crate from an early age. This simplifies the process because he already has a positive association regarding crates. Successful crate training reinforces this.

How to Crate Train Your Poodle

Your Poodle's crate should become part of his daily routine from the day you bring him home. Let him investigate it. Leave the door open, and hide a toy or treat in the back occasionally. He will begin to expect to find something good in there. Feeding him in the crate is another great way to instill a positive attitude.

Praise your Poodle by using a special phrase when he enters on his own. When he seems comfortable inside the crate, close the door. If he sits calmly and quietly, let him out and praise him after ten minutes. If he immediately starts carrying on, ignore it. Don't let him out until he settles down. Many dogs will happily enter the crate for their dinner and immediately start carrying on when they have finished. This is not a habit you want to encourage. If you let him out in response to this behavior, it will escalate.

Gradually increase his crate time up to two hours. Adult dogs can comfortably remain crated for eight hours, allowing you to get a good night's sleep. He should be mentally equipped to respond to confinement by playing with a toy or taking a nap—and have enough bladder and bowel control to avoid having accidents in his crate. However, never leave him in the crate until he is forced to relieve himself in there. He will have no choice but to overcome his natural

A well-trained dog is a pleasure to live with.

SENIOR DOG TIP

Training Techniques for the Older Dog

Dogs remain capable of learning new things throughout their lives. Training an older Poodle is easier in some ways and possibly more complicated in others than training a puppy or young adult. Older dogs are naturally more calm and focused but are more likely to be set in their ways, and training may actually consist mostly of retraining. Replacing a bad habit, such as barking nonstop while dinner is prepared, with a good one, like sitting quietly, can take time. Be patient and consistent even when you feel as if you are making no progress. Your senior Poodle's capacity to focus and override ingrained habits really will improve with time and practice.

instinct to keep his sleeping area clean. That habit is hard to discourage and will undermine housetraining.

Puppies usually learn to sleep through the night without a bathroom break by three months of age. To promote this habit, don't feed your dog too close to bedtime, and make sure

that he is emptied out before going to bed. If he does wake you needing to be let out during the night, make sure that he has the opportunity. If he just needed to potty, he should go back to sleep after relieving himself.

Housetraining

Just like crate training, housetraining builds on a dog's natural inclination to keep his surroundings clean. Puppies begin to exhibit this behavior as soon as they can walk. Good breeders make sure that they have the opportunity to follow this instinct before they even leave the whelping box. As they get older, their territory is gradually expanded. If you follow the same procedure after bringing your Poodle home, housetraining should be uneventful.

How to Housetrain Your Poodle

Whether your Poodle is a new puppy or a trained adult, implement and reinforce a routine as soon he arrives. Teach him where and when he is supposed to relieve himself. Don't complicate things for him by giving him unsupervised time and space. You should have decided on a workable housetraining schedule prior to his arrival. This might include taking him out before and after work and making arrangements for a family member or dog walker to see to this during the day. Whether you plan to train him to eliminate indoors or outdoors, he must have a conveniently accessible spot for this.

Accompany your Poodle to his spot at regular, scheduled intervals, and stay with him until he relieves himself. Immediately reward him with praise and treats. It may help to use a key phrase like "go potty," but don't give him so much attention that he gets distracted from what he is there for. And give him at least 10 or 15 minutes to eliminate. If he does not relieve himself by then, don't assume that he doesn't need to. Confine him to his crate or gated area for half an hour, and repeat the procedure until you have success. This is time consuming and occasionally frustrating, but it works.

You usually can predict when a dog needs to go out by his body language. The most common signs are sniffing and circling. If your Poodle exhibits any of these behaviors, calmly take him to his designated potty spot and reward him when he eliminates there.

Housetraining Accidents

If your Poodle has an accident, berating him won't help unless you catch him in the act. If this occurs, sternly tell him "No" and immediately take him to the right spot. Frightening or intimidating him may have the opposite effect and may prolong the entire training process.

Toy Poodles have a reputation for being more difficult to housetrain than Minis and Standards, but they are, in fact, just as intelligent. Lax training is usually the problem because owners are more reluctant to enforce rules with a tiny dog. This gives the dog mixed messages and a higher-than-average number of opportunities to have accidents. A puddle or pile from a tiny dog may not be immediately noticed, and he can get into a very bad habit before it is.

Dogs respond to the state of their environment, so telltale reminders of past accidents provide a constant lure for your puppy to do it again. This includes keeping their potty area clean and scrupulously removing all traces of an accident in the house. Otherwise, it will serve a constant reminder to your dog to use that spot again. Baking soda

Clicker Training

A clicker simplifies all types of training by streamlining the reward phase. Once he makes this connection, your Poodle will associate the clicker sound with an impending reward in any situation and respond with focused anticipation.

Start by simply clicking the clicker and giving a reward. Vary the time and place, and have other family members do it too. Very quickly, your dog will expect his reward every time he hears the click. Use this response to shape his behavior. For instance, tell him "Fido, come." When he starts toward you, click to reinforce the response and follow up with praise and a treat.

or enzyme odor neutralizer works to remove odors from rugs and upholstery.

Basic Commands

Poodles are smart but sensitive. The secret to training your Poodle, then, is to convince him that he wants to comply with your wishes. Training won't succeed unless you both enjoy the process as much as the results.

Come

The first and most important word to teach your Poodle is "come." It can save his life if he ever slips his lead or accidentally gets loose. Chasing a loose dog simply encourages him to run farther and faster. Instead, reinforce his natural instinct to follow you, the pack leader, by teaching him to come on command. Never call your Poodle to you to punish or berate him; if you do, he will be less likely to come to you in emergency situations.

How to Teach Come

To teach *come*, get down to your dog's eye level and use a soft encouraging voice to tell him "Fido, come." If necessary, entice him with toys, treats, or beckoning gestures. Praise him lavishly as soon as he approaches, and have a treat ready when he reaches you. Do this every day, varying the time and place. If possible, have other family members practice with him too.

Sit

Teaching your Poodle to reliably sit on command has the added benefit of helping him focus his attention. This is a huge step in the training process. Teaching him to sit on command will further enhance his powers of concentration, and it's also a great way to prevent him from jumping on guests or trying to snatch your sandwich off the kitchen table.

The come *command can save your dog's life if he gets loose or is in a dangerous situation.*

How to Teach Sit

To teach *sit*, call your Poodle and praise him when he comes, but don't get him too keyed up. Show him that you have a treat in your hand. Coax him into a sitting position by holding it above his nose. He will have to raise his head and lean back to follow your hand. (To lure a Toy Poodle into sitting, you need to kneel down.) As soon as his rump starts to descend, tell him "Sit" and give the reward.

Lying down is a vulnerable position for a dog, making the down *command a bit more difficult to teach than other commands.*

An alternative method is to give the command to sit, followed by praise or a treat whenever you see your dog sit, which is something he normally does hundreds of times each day. Whichever method you choose, he will form a connection between the word and the action.

Stay

When your Poodle has reliably learned *come* and *sit*, you can combine these lessons to prevent him from getting into mischief while you are doing everyday tasks, like talking on the phone or making dinner.

How to Teach Stay

It's usually easier to have your dog wear a leash when introducing the *stay* command. Tell him to come and sit. Reward him, but don't let him rise from the *sit* position. Show him that you have another treat. Tell him "Stay," and wait a few seconds. If he remains in place, use a different command like *okay t*o signal when he can get up. Don't expect him to stay more than a few seconds at first. If he moves immediately, put him back into the *sit* position and try again. A simultaneous vocal and hand gesture,

with arm outstretched, sometimes helps to reinforce the idea. Gradually increase the time before you give the reward, and begin backing a few steps away. In time, your Poodle should respond to your *sit-stay* command from across the room.

Down

Once your Poodle masters the *sit-stay*, he will have a far greater ability to focus on training and to ignore distractions. This makes a big difference when teaching the *down* command. Dogs naturally feel vulnerable in this position and are therefore more likely to be reluctant to comply. A good training rapport, built on past successes, will minimize this.

How to Teach Down

To teach *down*, put your dog into a *sit-stay* and show him a treat in your hand. Lower your hand, and his head should follow until he must lie down to reach the treat. As soon as he starts doing that, tell him "Down," and reward and praise him. If he has trouble with this command—and some dogs do—break it into smaller parts, rewarding each step as he gradually lowers his head and body and finally lies down.

Walk Nicely on Leash

Every dog needs to know how to walk politely on lead without lagging behind, pulling ahead, or tripping you. Even a Toy Poodle can become a "menace on the road" without leash manners. The easiest method is never to let your Poodle form bad habits in the first place, so maintaining an even pace on a loose leash should be encouraged as soon as you start his leash training. If it's too late for that, don't worry—you still can train your dog to walk nicely on a leash.

How to Teach Walk Nicely on Leash

First, you will need a pocket full of bite-sized treats. Dole these out regularly as your Poodle keeps pace with you. Praise him constantly when he walks at the desired pace, but never jerk the lead or yell at him when he doesn't. Many dogs reflexively respond to that by pulling even harder. If he forges ahead or lags behind, immediately stop and reverse directions. He will be forced to match your pace to get his reward.

Trick Training

Learning tricks can be one of your Poodle's most valuable training experiences. In contrast to formal training, tricks encourage a fun attitude. Trick training also can be an ongoing way to enhance your relationship with your dog. Once he discovers the approval potential of a good repertoire of tricks, don't be surprised if he stages his own spontaneous performances!

Shake Hands

Most dogs instinctively lift a paw toward you for attention. Whenever you notice your Poodle doing this on his own, tell him "Shake hands," say "Yes" to mark the behavior, and reward.

Sit Up

Once he has mastered *shake hands*, give that command, reward him, and then gently lift his other front paw. Most Poodles

can easily balance themselves in this position. As soon as he does, tell him "Sit up," say "Yes," and reward.

Dancing

Poodles are also experts at standing and walking on their hind legs. Most do this without any lessons. Be ready to reinforce this by telling him "Fido, dance" whenever he does it on his own. Say "Yes" and reward the behavior. While he is in that position, hold a treat over his nose and encourage him to take a few steps. You will be amazed at how long he can remain standing and walking on two legs.

Finding a Professional Trainer

Professional advice can be a tremendous aid in your Poodle's training, or it can undermine all your work. Dog trainers vary enormously in skill, experience, and philosophy. Regardless of whether you are seeking individualized instruction or a class, the trainer's approach is paramount.

A good trainer is flexible and open-minded. Every dog/handler team is different, and training is never "one size fits all." Beware of a trainer who rigidly adheres to a single method or who hesitates to try alternative techniques. Often, dogs who are labeled as stubborn or stupid respond readily to a different approach.

Groomers, vets, and local kennel clubs can usually direct you to trainers in your area. For more information on how to find a trainer, visit the Association of Pet Dog Trainers (APDT) at www.apdt.com.

Training is immensely rewarding, and many Poodle owners go on to try more challenging endeavors such as competitive obedience and agility. The important thing to remember is to keep it fun. This becomes especially important when you enter advanced competitive training. Winning is great but never compares to the satisfaction of forging a strong bond with your dog.

Poodles are naturally intelligent and so take easily to a variety of tricks, such as shaking hands.

Chapter 7

In the

Doghouse

The day your Poodle stepped into your life probably included daydreams about your wonderful future together. However, these imagined possibilities probably didn't include replacing the drapes, replanting the back yard, or dealing with irate neighbors.

Most canine behavior problems become obvious during adolescence. Puppies have ceased to be tiny, cute, and manageable, and owners stop clinging to the hope that bad behavior is merely a temporary phase that will be outgrown. Habits that are truly vexing in a ten-month-old puppy often stem from minor issues that were neglected many months earlier.

You can't put your dog into a time machine and revise the past, but behavior modification and retraining can resolve many of these problems if you are willing to do the work. Training the second time around is a greater challenge, though. Unwanted habits must be discouraged and replaced by desirable ones, which translates into lots of time, patience, repetition, and reinforcement—but it can be done!

Causes of Problem Behaviors

The first step in revising undesirable behavior is to identify the cause—and that does not include labeling Fido as an incorrigible canine delinquent. No matter how unusual or random a dog's actions may seem, there is always an under-lying reason.

Is an undetected health problem causing secondary problem behaviors?

As we all know, a minor joint or back injury can cause excruciating pain without apparent visible symptoms. This may be the explanation if your Poodle suddenly becomes reluctant to walk on a lead or shies away from being groomed or petted. The connection between a health condition and a problem behavior is not always obvious, so discuss your Poodle's misbehavior with your vet to rule out the possibility that he's not feeling well.

Is he receiving sufficient daily exercise and attention?

Toy, Miniature, and Standard Poodles all need daily outdoor exercise. Putting your Poodle outside in the yard to amuse himself is

Positive training techniques can help to solve many problem behaviors.

not a satisfactory alternative. He needs daily walks, play sessions, and opportunities to socialize.

Is his diet adequate? Food allergies or dietary imbalances can have behavioral as well as physical ramifications, although the effects may not show up immediately.

Is something in his environment causing a problem? Again, this may not be obvious. Canine dominance struggles within the home can create considerable stress without escalating into an actual dogfight. Mixed messages from various human members of the family also can leave a dog hopelessly confused. The problem might even be something outside the home, such as a rowdy dog next door or a noisy construction job across the street.

If you are unable to trace your Poodle's problem to any of these possible internal or external factors, he may simply need some good old-fashioned remedial training.

Common Problem Behaviors

Common problem behaviors include excessive barking, chewing, digging, house soiling, dominance issues, fearfulness, and jumping up.

Barking (Excessive)

Puppies discover very early in life that barking, howling, crying, and whining get results—and these canine signals

FAMILY-FRIENDLY TIP

Building Trust

Every successful relationship between a child and a dog is built on mutual trust. Your Poodle learns that it's not okay to nip or growl at your child, and your child learns to treat the dog with love and respect. Under normal circumstances, this takes time and supervision.

Things become much more complicated if your Poodle suffers from a problem behavior because he cannot be relied on to react predictably or appropriately in certain situations. A child should never be encouraged to respond to a dog displaying erratic behavior. For instance, a child may have good intentions trying to reassure a fearful pet but could easily be bitten in a situation like that. Instead, explain the dog's problem so that your child can recognize the behavior when it occurs. Rather than trying to interact with the dog, the child should immediately tell you about it.

work equally well on humans. Don't fall into this trap. Dogs bark—and howl, whine, and cry—for many needless reasons. (Keep in mind, though, that some barking is normal, and it is unreasonable to expect your Poodle to ignore this natural instinct completely.) Some Poodles gain a reputation for excessive barking, thanks to owners failing to keep this behavior within bounds. Responding to unnecessary barking, intentionally or otherwise, will turn it into an ingrained habit before you know it.

Solution

If your Poodle habitually barks to demand his walk, his dinner, or your dinner, don't cater to this behavior. It will get worse. Instead, redirect him by telling him "Sit, stay," and consistently reward the behavior you want to encourage.

Dogs instinctively react by barking when they perceive a threat in their environment. That's a normal response. However, it should not continue for 45 minutes after the doorbell rings. If your Poodle does happen to get carried away, he should stop when told to do so. Training him to speak on command can help teach him to be quiet. To teach this, do something that usually prompts him to bark, like ringing the doorbell. When he barks, tell him "Speak," and reward him. He will quickly make the connection because he's being rewarded for something he loves to do. Once he reliably barks on command, work on "quiet." After telling him "Speak," say "Quiet." He may ignore you, but he cannot bark forever. Offer him a treat because it's impossible to eat and bark simultaneously. As soon as he stops, repeat the command and give the reward. This can take some practice, but it is worth it.

Prolonged barking at environmental stimuli also can be due to boredom. In that case, you need to give your Poodle more interesting pastimes than barking at passing cars.

Inadequately socialized dogs can be prone to nervous barking at anything unfamiliar. If your dog has not been trained to tolerate spending time alone, he may resort to chronic barking to quell his anxiety. Revising these habits requires slow acclimation until he can comfortably tolerate strange sights and sounds or separation from you. It is possible to curb this habit by slowly introducing a dog to fearful situations until he becomes comfortable. A severe case may require the guidance

Provide your dog with safe, fun chew toys to prevent him from chewing on something undesirable or dangerous.

of a certified behaviorist; an inexperienced or inept trainer can easily make matters worse.

Chewing

Chewing consistently ranks among the all-time favorite canine hobbies. Most dogs happily devote hours on end to chewing, and almost none are willing to quit the habit.

Solution

Rather than fight a losing battle, just accept it. Recreational chewing can solve problems for both of you. Provide a good selection of safe, enticing chew toys to keep your dog happy and occupied when you are busy. Make things interesting by rotating his toys so that he has a few different ones each week. Many Poodles love stuffable toys that require ingenuity to get at the treat inside.

Puppies are likely to go through a phase of intensive chewing during teething, but this needn't be accompanied by rampant destruction. In addition to the urge to chew, a puppy has lots of energy and a short attention span. You must supervise to prevent unwanted chewing. Don't put temptation in your dog's way by leaving him alone with your Louis XIV chairs and designer handbag. When you catch him chewing something he should not have, redirect him to his

To keep your dog from digging, supervise him when he's outdoors.

toys. Don't punish him because you forgot to close the door or pick up your things. Punishment will increase his anxiety, and he will turn to chewing to relieve it.

Digging

Some dogs have a strong natural instinct to dig, but almost any dog will resort to this habit to relieve boredom. It's self-reinforcing because it feels good, and dogs easily learn it from each other. And it isn't always limited to digging holes in the back yard—the couch cushions work just as well.

Solution

Discouraging the habit requires a combination of better supervision and redirecting the digging to something nondestructive but equally satisfying. Digging is a self-reinforcing habit that

Finding the Lost Dog

2 If possible, organize search parties to simultaneously cover different parts of the neighborhood by car and on foot while maintaining cell phone communication. Don't be shy about asking mail carriers, gardeners, delivery people, and dog walkers if they have seen the dog running around the neighborhood. You can get some great leads this way. Many dogs go just a few blocks before seeking a hiding place. Look in shrubbery, under cars, and behind garden sheds.

3 Notify all local animal-related businesses, groomers, vets, feed stores, pet shops, shelters, and local breeders that your Poodle is missing. Local businesses are also great places to post your flyers.

4 Don't be quick to give up the search. Keep expanding the territory. Place classified and Internet ads, and regularly call shelters to make sure that they have your dog's description and microchip number.

Every owner's worst nightmare is discovering the gate unlatched and the dog missing. Although it's horrible to contemplate, having a game plan ready maximizes your odds of getting your Poodle back. Even if he is microchipped, tattooed, and/or licensed, an ID tag bearing your phone number remains your best insurance. Very likely, someone will find him before he wanders too far, and if possible, will immediately call and notify you.

Don't waste a minute when you discover that your dog is missing. Include the following steps in your search:

1 Immediately print a sheaf of flyers bearing your dog's picture, name, brief description, the time and place he was last seen, contact telephone numbers, and the offer of a reward. Bring a staple gun, and post the flyers as you search.

can be tough to discourage, so you need to get your Poodle's mind on something else. Take him for a walk, play ball with him, or if you don't have the energy for that, give him an irresistible chew toy to keep him occupied.

Your Poodle's schedule needs revamping if he devotes large blocks of unsupervised time to alleviating his boredom by digging. If you are forced to leave him alone during the workday, a day care program or dog walking service may be the answer.

House Soiling

Almost all housetraining relapses are due to inadequate training the first time around. The fact that Fido reliably used the doggy door a few times does not signify that his training is complete. In fact, supervision and reinforcement should be continued long after he seems reliably housetrained. Moving to a new home or making abrupt changes in his typical routine also can trigger house soiling problems.

Solution

Regardless of the reason, you must reinstate the entire housetraining routine and stick to it faithfully. Take your dog to his elimination spot at designated times, supervise until he does what he's there for, and always reward him. His access to the house must be restricted during retraining. If he has targeted a specific room, keep him out of there altogether. Thoroughly clean all soiled areas to eradicate stains and odors. As he becomes more reliable, gradually expand his territory but continue supervising closely. Otherwise, you may face the possibility of going through the whole routine a third time.

In some cases, a reliably trained dog will begin territorial marking when he reaches adolescence. Neutering is not a guaranteed preventive. Reinforcing housetraining rules often helps to curb this behavior. For recalcitrant customers, bellybands or panties are often effective to discourage it.

If your formerly housetrained Poodle begins having frequent accidents, have him checked by your vet to rule out possible physical causes, like intestinal parasites, diabetes, or bladder stones.

Dominant Behavior

Dogs use dominance to protect their rank and resources within their pack, and some figure out that these tactics work equally well on humans. Every puppy finds himself a niche within your pack as he becomes part of your family. A dominant puppy develops a natural drive to upgrade his status at around eight to nine months of age. He may start acting possessive, territorial, and intolerant of strangers like guests or delivery people that enter the home. This might not actually become a problem until adulthood, when temperament, hormones, adult size, and poor training combine to create a monster.

Far more common than natural dominance is opportunistic dominance. Nearly every dog is capable of this, because opportunism is part of the canine personality. Opportunistic dogs are not dominant by nature, but they become encouraged to demand higher status in the family through the treatment they receive from their owners. Eventually, they start experimenting with the behaviors associated with dominance, like ignoring commands, disobeying certain family members, objecting to being petted or groomed, or guarding food and toys. Repeatedly getting away with

this further enhances the dog's confidence, and the problem becomes self-perpetuating.

Solution

A consistent routine will encourage your Poodle to accept you as his pack leader because you control the resources. Obedience training also can help to reinforce his understanding of his place in the family pack. If you have a Poodle puppy, start this training by five to six months of age—after you have formed a strong bond with him. Forming a strong bond with an adult may take a little more time, but formal training is not going to be effective without communication and trust.

Assert yourself as pack leader by taking control of your dog's toys, food, walks, and attention. Ask him to comply with a simple command, such as *sit*, *down*, or *stay*, before giving him access to those things. Also, never allow a dominant dog to beg at the table. Feeding him on demand during your mealtime greatly enhances his perception of himself as pack leader. Having access to the furniture or sleeping in your bed can send the same message as well. His remedial training should include eating and sleeping in a crate. Neutering can also help, but it will not produce

The Expert Knows

When to Seek Professional Help

Many canine problem behaviors readily respond to retraining, but certain problems are better managed with professional help. If your Poodle is extremely fearful, dominant, or aggressive, seek the advice of a skilled behaviorist. Attempting to revise these behaviors on your own may only make them worse. You also can risk being bitten if you don't know what you are doing.

major changes, because a large component of dominance is learned.

Fearfulness

Fearful experiences are part of every puppy's learning process. When frightened, he may overreact by passively freezing, cowering, shaking, whining, backing away, or running. Puppies usually learn to overcome irrational fears through consistent training and socialization, but not always. A naturally timid puppy requires extra encouragement to explore and socialize, and he is unlikely to confront challenges otherwise. Even a confident pup will become fearful if denied opportunities to learn and explore. It is also possible for a puppy to be permanently traumatized by a single terrifying event. Regardless of the reason, if these problems are not sorted out during puppyhood, they will become a routine response to unfamiliar situations.

Solution

Inadequate socialization or traumatic experiences can make a dog overly fearful of anything strange or challenging. A timid puppy simply requires socialization that is more consistent. However, the process must be geared toward what he can handle. Always present new (potentially scary) things in a highly positive manner. Puppies seek reassurance from their pack leader, so you must impart the message that new things are fun and safe. For example, whenever your dog remains responsive to you despite displaying signs of anxiety, reward this reaction. Positive reinforcement throughout this process won't leave his reactions to chance. Above all else, be sensitive of his limited coping skills, but remember that overprotectiveness is equally defeating.

The same methods can be used to help a fearful adult overcome this problem. It may take more time, though, because adults are slower to revise ingrained behavior patterns.

Jumping Up

Poodles are incredibly agile, and many of them feel quite comfortable in a vertical position.

If your dog jumps up, try teaching him an alternative behavior, such as the sit *command.*

Therefore jumping can be a tough habit to stop. Keep this in mind before you start encouraging your dog to jump up to give you a kiss or get a cookie, because behavior that seems cute and harmless in a puppy can become quite annoying in an adult. A dog is also likely to become extremely confused if you suddenly start reprimanding him for something that formerly elicited praiseand attention.

Solution

Prevention is key; in other words, if you don't want your adult Poodle jumping, don't let him do it when he is little.

If little Fido has indeed grown up to be a large, curly-haired jumping bean, curbing that habit requires dedicated effort. Every person he comes in contact with must reinforce the "four on the floor" rule. That includes all family members, his dog walker, groomer, and the receptionist at the vet's office. If he continues to get a positive reaction from a single person, he won't be inclined to stop.

Because jumping up is a reactive, adrenaline-fueled reaction, loud verbal or physical reprimands often increase a dog's jumping frenzy. If you yell at him, knee him in the chest, step on his toes, or yank on his leash, he will probably tune you out and keep bouncing. Instead, before he has a chance to launch himself, grab his collar with both hands and firmly but calmly tell him to sit. Praise him for obeying, but don't go overboard and get him all keyed up again. Everyone who customarily gets the vertical greeting from your dog must consistently reinforce this message.

Finding a Behaviorist

A canine behaviorist specializes in interpreting and modifying complex behavior issues that don't readily respond to conventional training.

SENIOR DOG TIP

Older Dogs and Problem Behaviors

Modifying the habits of an older dog can be a challenge, but it's not impossible. Dogs retain the potential to learn new things throughout their lives, and the actual training process is basically the same for dogs of any age. However, an older dog may need more encouragement to stay motivated and plenty of positive reinforcement to override old habits and accept new ones. You may need to experiment with various training methods to discover what he responds to best, like using praise, food, verbal signals, hand signals, clicker training, or something else. Be patient, persistent, and creative, and you will see results.

Although there are many excellent practitioners, the field is also populated with a few questionable individuals. This is an inexact science, and certification is not a prerequisite for anyone in the business.

A true behaviorist has either a Ph.D. in applied animal behavior or board certification as a veterinary behaviorist. Behavioral consultants, on the other hand, are not licensed or required to meet any particular qualifications. This can make it difficult to evaluate someone's ability based on claims and credentials. Theoretical knowledge does not invariably translate into practical skill. Impressive qualifications (and high fees) should be matched by extensive hands-on experience.

Long-term experience is good, but this should not include outdated methods. Competent professionals utilize ongoing education to learn the latest techniques and principles. How many dogs has this individual worked with? Ask for references, especially from the owners of other dogs this person has successfully treated. Don't hesitate to ask direct questions about the possible duration and costs of treatment. Request detailed information about the techniques that will be used to help your dog, and ask what will be recommended if this method fails.

A canine behaviorist can interpret and modify problem behaviors that don't readily respond to conventional training.

For more information on behaviorists and how to find one, visit the following websites:

- www.animalbehavior.org (Animal Behavior Society)
- www.iaabc.org (International Association of Animal Behavior Consultants)
- www.veterinarybehaviorists.org (American College of Veterinary Behaviorists)

No one plans to cope with problem behaviors when they acquire a dog. However, the majority of them can be resolved with creativity, practice, and patience. In the end, it's a fair trade-off for the emotional support and unconditional love your Poodle provides.

Chapter 8

Stepping Out

Extracurricular activities are more accessible to dog owners today than ever before. No matter where you live, there is something tailor made for your interests and your Poodle's talents. Poodles are good at so many things that your problem will be choosing which one to try. They can compete for AKC titles in events such as conformation, agility, and obedience. Over the years, Poodles have also garnered praise as therapy dogs, and if you prefer to stray from the beaten path, they also excel at pastimes like swimming.

Agility

Agility debuted at the Crufts dog show in Great Britain in 1978. It was modeled after equestrian show jumping and was originally intended as entertainment. It immediately sparked worldwide interest and proved equally appealing as a sport. Agility has proven to be tremendously popular with exhibitors of both large and small breeds, and Poodles take to it like ducks to water.

Although it's fun, agility is not for the fainthearted. This sport requires considerable mental and physical dexterity. Handlers must keep pace with their dogs, running full speed while directing them through a course of 16 to 20 obstacles such as tables, tunnels, chutes, hurdles, A-frames, and weave poles. Entrants receive a detailed map of the course and obstacles in advance and have an opportunity to familiarize themselves with the layout during a pre-competition "walk through." Competitions are broken into five size divisions and three expertise levels, Novice, Open, and Excellent.

Agility is enormously rewarding even if you don't aspire to lofty goals.

Most Poodles react like kids at a playground when they first see an agility course. Your Poodle must be a year old to enter AKC agility competitions, but many clubs offer informal events for novices and casual participants. Get your vet's approval before starting, and learn the ropes by enrolling in a basic agility class.

Conformation (Dog Shows)

Conformation is the oldest and most well-known dog sport, and glamorous Poodles in show trims are the breed most often associated with it.

The competition by which a dog becomes a champion or wins Best in Show is conducted as

Many Poodles prove adept at a variety of activities and sports such as agility.

a process of elimination. At the first level, Poodles compete against members of their own variety—Toy, Miniature, and Standard—in separate classes for males and females, puppies and adults, and champions and non-champions. Each dog is assessed on structural soundness, temperament, and features of Poodle type such as coat texture and eye shape. The most important class at this stage is Best of Variety, where the best Toy, Miniature, and Standard Poodle are chosen. Those three dogs are then evaluated against the best representative of the other breeds in each respective group. Minis and Standards compete in the Non-Sporting Group, and Toys compete in the Toy Group. The seven group winners then enter the final phase of the elimination process, where the ultimate Best in Show winner emerges from hundreds or thousands of dogs.

It requires substantial time, work, and money to achieve success at this level. If you want to show your Poodle in conformation, find an experienced mentor to guide you. Poodles are often

Sports and Safety

Sports are meant to help you keep fit and have fun with your Poodle, but your primary concern is keeping him safe. No matter how much he enjoys a sport, he cannot tell you if he is tired, sore, or feeling ill. Those judgment calls are your responsibility.

Get your vet's okay before starting your dog on any demanding exercise routine. Give him time to gradually build up his stamina. Include warm-up and cool-down time in every exercise session to prevent muscle strains. Make sure that he drinks water frequently during exercise, but never let him gulp an entire bowl of water at once or exercise soon after eating. This is especially important for Standards, to prevent bloat. Toy Poodles may benefit from a high-energy snack or glucose drink during a workout. If Toys engage in group activities, they should never be exposed to danger from larger dogs who may regard them as prey or accidentally jump on or step on them.

called a "handler's breed," meaning that most successful show dogs are presented by professionals. That doesn't mean that novices and owner/handlers cannot win. But the level of professionalism is extremely high, and you must know the ropes to succeed.

Enroll in a conformation training class to learn the basics. From ringside, the mechanics of showing a dog seem effortless. Learning how to pose a dog for examination and move him around the ring isn't difficult, but mastering the art of showcasing his

In conformation shows, a dog is judged against the standard for the breed.

are limited to a single breed, and almost every mid-size city has a group of devoted Poodle lovers. Meetups provide opportunities for both Poodles and their owners to socialize and make friends.

Meetups attract anywhere from 10 to 100 devoted Poodle lovers. Most take place at a public space, like dog parks or malls. Others are by invitation only, at locations ranging from bars and restaurants to someone's backyard. Owners exchange tips, discuss concerns, and, most of all, enjoy watching their Poodles run and play together. Many meetup groups start off informally. As they grow, they become more organized and sponsor charity fundraisers for Poodle rescue and educational programs on Poodle care.

Visit www.meetup.com to find a Poodle group in your area. If you can't find one, consider starting one of your own.

best features and disguising his faults is challenging.

Match shows are the next step in preparing for competition. Matches offer classes for puppies not yet old enough to enter real shows. Aspiring show dogs, handlers, and judges all attend match shows to hone their skills.

Contact local kennel clubs in your area to find out about conformation training classes and upcoming matches.

Meetups

Meetups are quickly becoming the premier dog/owner social activity. Unlike dog parks or day care, meetups

Obedience

Obedience became a competitive AKC event in 1936, and Poodles commanded attention in this sport immediately. It is often regarded as the most exacting canine activity for both handlers and dogs. The sport's mental and physical demands have made obedience the basis for agility, tracking, search and rescue, therapy work, and fieldwork.

Registered dogs more than six months of age can compete, including neutered Poodles and those with undocumented lineage or disqualifying faults. The competition consists of increasingly challenging exercises, beginning with basics like coming when called and working up to things like identifying and retrieving specific objects. The judge compares each dog's performance against the imagined concept of the ideal execution for each exercise. Each dog/handler team begins with 200 points, and deductions are made for errors. A dog must earn at least half the points allotted for each exercise, totaling a minimum of 170 for a qualifying score, and three qualifying scores under different judges are needed to earn a title. There are three levels of obedience: Novice, Open and Utility.

Swimming

Swimming is universally regarded as one of the best forms of exercise. Most Poodles love it thanks to their legacy of water dog ancestry. Your Poodle will probably relish a chance to enjoy his natural inclination and show off his ability, but always keep safety in mind.

Never let your dog take a dip unless you are certain the water is safe and swimming by dogs is permitted. In addition to some lakes and beaches, many dog parks have beaches or pools strictly for dogs. Watch your Poodle at

What to Pack

If your Poodle travels frequently, it may be easier to have a separate travel kit for him rather than rounding up everything every time you pack. This should include an extra leash, brush, dishes, bedding, clean-up supplies, a canine first-aid kit, and a supply of any prescription drugs he needs. Pack all his essentials, but be sensible about how much you can carry. For instance, bring only enough food and bottled water for immediate needs if you can purchase more on arrival. If traveling to a different climate, you may need special items like tick repellent and weather-related accessories.

Travel always increases the risk that a dog may become lost, so an ID tag attached to your Poodle's collar or harness is essential even if he is microchipped or tattooed. Always carry a couple of recent photos of him in case you need to mount a lost pet search.

all times while he is swimming. As much as he loves it, don't let him stay in long enough to become overtired.

Many Poodles have an affinity for water, making swimming an excellent way for your dog to get exercise and have fun.

Even an expert swimmer can go under if he becomes exhausted. It also may be advisable to give him a bath when you get home to remove traces of salt water, chlorine, or bacteria that may adhere to his coat.

Therapy

Canine therapy work evolved from a series of scientific studies conducted in the 1970s to objectively confirm that interacting with a dog could speed recovery by relieving the loneliness, stress, and depression of illness. Surprisingly, this research also showed that contact with dogs lowered blood pressure and cholesterol levels and triggered the release of endorphins. The Delta Society subsequently designed a training program to certify therapy dogs for this work. Today, more than 8,500 therapy dogs and handlers provide companionship to residents of nursing homes, hospitals, and rehabilitation centers all over the country.

Poodles are among the most popular breeds for this work. Their minimally shedding coat is unlikely to trigger an allergic reaction, and their loving, tolerant temperament is well suited to the demands of the job.

Therapy dog candidates must undergo basic obedience training and Canine Good Citizen certification before undergoing a 21-step evaluation program run by local therapy dog programs.

Travel

One of the biggest dilemmas of pet ownership is what to do with your dog when you travel. You could board him in a kennel or hire a dog sitter, but you are going to miss your dog if you leave him behind. With a little advance planning, you can bring him along to enjoy your adventures and keep you company.

Car Travel

Properly introducing young Bruno to car travel as a puppy can make the difference between loving or dreading car rides. Many dogs ride in the car only when going to the vet or groomer. This may lead to negative mental associations about it.

Begin familiarizing your dog to short trips, and make the experience fun. This will help to offset anxiety and prevent carsickness. If he is prone to carsickness, do not feed him before a trip. Natural remedies like ginger sometimes help, as can non-prescription travel sickness meds—but consult your vet before using them. Generally, carsickness diminishes as a dog becomes used to the routine.

An unsecured crate is a major cause of nervousness and upset stomach. For safety, your Poodle should ride in his crate, but it must be securely placed and not bouncing around when the car is moving. If he has trouble adjusting to riding in the crate, try a canine car seat or seat belt, but these usually work best for dogs who are somewhat accustomed

FAMILY-FRIENDLY TIP

Traveling With Your Poodle and Child

Minimizing stress and confusion is paramount when traveling with a child and a dog. Give yourself extra time for everything, especially the time needed to ensure a safe travel routine. Ask your child to help you make sure that seat belts are buckled and crate doors are latched. This will make the child feel more responsible and involved in the outcome of the trip. You can also ask her to help to keep track of the dog's things and make sure that he is calm and happy.

to car travel. He should never be loose in the car when it's moving or allowed to sit on your lap while you drive.

Air Travel

The documentation needed for air travel is frequently revised and can vary depending on your destination. Double-check requirements close to your departure date. Your Poodle must have a health certificate issued within seven days of departure, possibly an acclimation certificate, and a vaccination certificate. Always carry a duplicate set of your Poodle's health papers when traveling in case the originals are mislaid or lost with your luggage.

Most airlines permit Toy Poodles to travel in the cabin because they fit into a carrier stowed under the seat. Miniature and Standard Poodles must fly in the cargo hold. Either way, introduce your Poodle to his travel carrier well prior to the trip. Sedating a dog for travel can be risky and is not recommended.

Supplement the airline's baggage identification tags with your own labels detailing your flight number, dog's name and breed, your contact

FAMILY-FRIENDLY TIP

Traveling With Your Senior Poodle

Changes in routine or environment that would not stress a younger Poodle can be difficult for an older dog to accept. When traveling with your geriatric Poodle, adhere to his normal schedule as much as possible. A familiar toy or blanket can help him settle in and feel secure. If he needs a special diet, bring enough food for the duration of the trip. It also might be advisable to give him bottled rather than tap water when traveling, to prevent stomach upset. Make sure that he drinks enough water, especially during summer, to prevent dehydration. In addition, give him frequent breaks to stretch his legs and relieve himself. Older dogs are less able to cope with temperature extremes, so pack a crate fan or heating pad for him if necessary.

When traveling with your Poodle, make sure that he is comfortable and safe.

information at home and at your destination, and a label stating that the crate should not be opened by airline personnel. Be prepared to remove your dog and his bedding from his carrier for security inspection. Some airlines apply a seal to crate doors after check-in. If not, you can do this using zip ties or a padlock after his crate is inspected.

After boarding the plane, ask the flight crew to confirm that your Poodle also is on board. Insist on knowing this before the plane leaves the gate. Ask where and when pets will be available to be picked up upon arrival. If your dog seems agitated after the flight, don't take him out of his crate until you are in a safer location. Always attach his leash to his collar before allowing him out of a crate, car, or hotel room in any unfamiliar location.

Book a direct flight if possible when flying with your Poodle. Most airlines don't accept animals for shipment in extremely hot or cold weather. They may waive this rule or accept a dog with an acclimation certificate if the pet is traveling as excess baggage. It is safer yet to avoid flying with your Poodle during extreme weather, holidays, and weekends, when planes are more likely to be delayed, grounded, or rerouted.

Working Certificate

Any registered Poodle over six months old can earn a Poodle Club of America (PCA) Working Certificate (WC) and Working Certificate Excellent (WCX). The requirements are designed to demonstrate the Poodle's natural ability as a working hunting dog. Dogs must be able to locate game, accurately respond to directions, and retrieve birds from water. Poodles can fulfill these requirements by successfully completing an approved field test or hunt test or earning a working certificate from an approved retriever club.

The PCA also holds a WC/WCX trial in conjunction with their national specialty. Many hunt and retriever clubs also sponsor tests that Poodles can compete in to fulfill WC requirements. These events are limited to Miniature and Standard Poodles because of the size of birds that must be retrieved.

Poodles fit effortlessly into so many activities and environments thanks to their natural versatility. They truly are ideal companions!

Resources

Associations and Organizations

Breed Clubs

American Kennel Club (AKC)
5580 Centerview Drive
Raleigh, NC 27606
Telephone: (919) 233-9767
Fax: (919) 233-3627
E-mail: info@akc.org
www.akc.org

Canadian Kennel Club (CKC)
89 Skyway Avenue, Suite 100
Etobicoke, Ontario M9W 6R4
Telephone: (416) 675-5511
Fax: (416) 675-6506
E-mail: information@ckc.ca
www.ckc.ca

Federation Cynologique Internationale (FCI)
Secretariat General de la FCI
Place Albert 1er, 13
B – 6530 Thuin
Belqique
www.fci.be

The Kennel Club
1 Clarges Street
London
W1J 8AB
Telephone: 0870 606 6750
Fax: 0207 518 1058
www.the-kennel-club.org.uk

United Kennel Club (UKC)
100 E. Kilgore Road
Kalamazoo, MI 49002-5584
Telephone: (269) 343-9020
Fax: (269) 343-7037
E-mail: pbickell@ukcdogs.com
www.ukcdogs.com

Pet Sitters

National Association of Professional Pet Sitters
15000 Commerce Parkway, Suite C
Mt. Laurel, New Jersey 08054
Telephone: (856) 439-0324
Fax: (856) 439-0525
E-mail: napps@ahint.com
www.petsitters.org

Pet Sitters International
201 East King Street
King, NC 27021-9161
Telephone: (336) 983-9222
Fax: (336) 983-5266
E-mail: info@petsit.com
www.petsit.com

Rescue Organizations and Animal Welfare Groups

American Society for the Prevention of Cruelty to Animals (ASPCA)
424 E. 92nd Street
New York, NY 10128-6804
Telephone: (212) 876-7700
www.aspca.org

Royal Society for the Prevention of Cruelty to Animals (RSPCA)
Telephone: 0870 3335 999
Fax: 0870 7530 284
www.rspca.org.uk

Therapy

Delta Society
875 124th Ave NE, Suite 101
Bellevue, WA 98005
Telephone: (425) 226-7357
Fax: (425) 235-1076
E-mail: info@deltasociety.org
www.deltasociety.org

Therapy Dogs International (TDI)
88 Bartley Road
Flanders, NJ 07836
Telephone: (973) 252-9800
Fax: (973) 252-7171
E-mail: tdi@gti.net
www.tdi-dog.org

Training

Association of Pet Dog Trainers (APDT)
150 Executive Center Drive Box 35
Greenville, SC 29615
Telephone: (800) PET-DOGS
Fax: (864) 331-0767
E-mail: information@apdt.com
www.apdt.com

National Association of Dog Obedience Instructors (NADOI)
PMB 369
729 Grapevine Hwy.
Hurst, TX 76054-2085
www.nadoi.org

Veterinary and Health Resources

American Animal Hospital Association (AAHA)
P.O. Box 150899
Denver, CO 80215-0899
Telephone: (303) 986-2800
Fax: (303) 986-1700
E-mail: info@aahanet.org
www.aahanet.org/index.cfm

American Holistic Veterinary Medical Association (AHVMA)
2218 Old Emmorton Road
Bel Air, MD 21015
Telephone: (410) 569-0795
Fax: (410) 569-2346
E-mail: office@ahvma.org
www.ahvma.org

American Veterinary Medical Association (AVMA)
1931 North Meacham Road – Suite 100
Schaumburg, IL 60173
Telephone: (847) 925-8070
Fax: (847) 925-1329
E-mail: avmainfo@avma.org
www.avma.org

ASPCA Animal Poison Control Center
1717 South Philo Road, Suite 36
Urbana, IL 61802
Telephone: (888) 426-4435
www.aspca.org

British Veterinary Association (BVA)
7 Mansfield Street
London
W1G 9NQ
Telephone: 020 7636 6541
Fax: 020 7436 2970
E-mail: bvahq@bva.co.uk
www.bva.co.uk

Index

Note: **Boldfaced** numbers indicate illustrations.

Index

Acknowledgments

I would like to thank Lucille Curzon (Caprice Poodles) for taking the time to read my manuscript and for generously sharing her extensive knowledge of the breed.

About the Author

Freelance artist and writer Amy Fernandez has bred Chinese Cresteds since 1980. She has authored several books, including Dog Breeding as a Fine Art, winner of the prestigious DWAA Presidential Award of Excellence. She writes a monthly column for *Top Notch Toys* and writes for *Dog World*, *Popular Dogs*, the AKC *Gazette*, AKC *Family Dog*, and *Dogs in Review*. Her *Dogs in Review* historical series won the 2004 and 2005 Elsworth Howell Award. She is president of the Dog Writers Association of America, president of the Xoloitzcuintli Club of America, and editor of the "Xolo News." Her artwork can be viewed at www.amyfernandez.com.

Photo Credits

Manuel Abinuman Jr. (Shutterstock): 62
Mary Bloom: 112 (author photo)
Paulette Braun: 56, 84
Parpalea Catalin (Shutterstock): front cover, 12
Stuart Cuss (Shutterstock): 82
Jaimie Duplass (Shutterstock): 98
Tim Elliot (Shutterstock): 61, 75
Cate Frost (Shutterstock): 52
Racheal Grazias (Shutterstock): 85
Gertjan Hooijer (Shutterstock): 60
Andrew Kua Seng How (Shutterstock): 86
Eric Isselée (Shutterstock): 24 (dog)
Michael Ledray (Shutterstock): 72
Robert A. Mansker (Shutterstock): 104
Gabor Palkovics (Shutterstock): 38
pixshots (Shutterstock): 4
Quayside (Shutterstock): 58, 92
Chin Kit Sen (Shutterstock): 14, back cover (second from top)
Tootles: back cover (bottom)
Aleksandar Vozarevic (Shutterstock): 24 (bowl)
All other photos courtesy of Isabelle Francais and T.F.H. archives.